EXETER MEDIEVAL ENGLISH TEXTS AND STUDIES
General Editors: Marion Glasscoe and M.J. Swanton

T0313431

CYNEWULF'S
JULIANA

Edited by

ROSEMARY WOOLF

UNIVERSITY
of
EXETER
PRESS

First published in
Methuen's Old English Library, London, 1955

Reprinted with revisions
by the University of Exeter 1977, 1981

This revised edition published in 1993 by
University of Exeter Press
Reed Hall
Streatham Drive
Exeter EX4 4QR
UK

www.exeterpress.co.uk

Printed digitally since 2001

ISBN 978 0 85989 421 0

Printed and bound by CPI Group (UK) Ltd, Croydon, CR0 4YY

PREFACE

A NEW edition of *Juliana* has for some time been required in order to replace the now antiquated work of Strunk. In my attempt to provide a substitute which may be more satisfactory, I am grateful to Mrs M. 'Espinasse and Mr A.T.W. Green for reading and commenting on the Introduction in manuscript, to Professor A.H. Smith and Professor F. Norman, who, as General Editors of the Series, have given me much useful and necessary advice in adapting my edition to the requirements of Methuen's Old English Library, and, above all, to Professor C.L. Wrenn, under whose invaluable guidance I originally undertook the work.

ROSEMARY WOOLF

UNIVERSITY OF HULL
1954

NOTE TO THIS EDITION

THIS EDITION incorporates revisions made by the late Rosemary Woolf prior to her death in 1978. In addition the bibliography has been recast and brought up to date.

MJS, EXETER 1993

CONTENTS

ABBREVIATIONS

When an author's name is cited alone further details of his work will be found in the Bibliography.

BBA . . .	*Bonner Beiträge zur Anglistik*
Brooks . .	*Andreas and the Fates of the Apostles*, ed. K. R. Brooks, 1961
BT . . .	J. Bosworth and T. N. Toller, *An Anglo-Saxon Dictionary*, 1898, *Supplement*, 1921
Bülbring . .	K. D. Bülbring, *Altenglisches Elementarbuch*, 1902
Campbell. .	A. Campbell, *Old English Grammar*, 1959
EWS . . .	Early West Saxon
ed. . . .	edited by
GK . . .	C. W. M. Grein, *Sprachsatz der angelsächsischen Dichter*, neu herausgeben von J. J. Köhler, 1914
Gradon . .	*Cynewulf's Elene*, ed. P. O. E. Gradon, 1958
GW . . .	C. W. M. Grein and R. P. Wülcker, *Bibliothek der angelsächsischen Poesie* III, 1897
JEGPh . .	*Journal of English and Germanic Philology*
Jente . .	Richard Jente, *Die mythologischen Ausdrücke im altenglischen Wortschatz*, 1921
Klaeber . .	*Beowulf* ed. F. Klaeber (3rd ed.), 1941
ME . . .	Middle English
MED . . .	*Middle English Dictionary*
MLN . . .	*Modern Language Notes*
NED . . .	*New English Dictionary*
OE . . .	Old English
O.N. . . .	Old Norse
PMLA . .	*Publications of the Modern Language Association of America*
RES . . .	*Review of English Studies*
Sievers . .	E. Sievers, *Altenglische Grammatik, Neubearbeitet von* K. Brunner, 1942
Vita . . .	'Acta auctore anonymo', the earliest extant life of Juliana, in the *Acta Sanctorum*, ed. Iohannes Bollandus and Godefridus Herschenius, *Februarius*, tom. II 873 ff.
WSax . .	West Saxon
Wright . .	J. Wright, *Old English Grammar* (2nd ed.), 1914

INTRODUCTION

I. Manuscript

The Old English life of Juliana is preserved between the *Phoenix* and the *Wanderer* on folios 65ᵇ–76ᵃ of the *Exeter Book*. This manuscript is the largest and most varied in content of the four codices of Old English poetry. It was given to Exeter Cathedral, where it still remains, by Leofric, Bishop of Devon and Cornwall, who died in 1072. During the course of time it has been seriously damaged by charring, stains, and the loss of folios. As a result of the latter there are two gaps in the text of *Juliana*, after ll. 288 and 558, which conclude folios 69ᵇ and 73ᵇ respectively. A comparison of the Old English poem with the *Vita* suggests that not more than one leaf is missing at either place (it would contain about 45 lines of writing, approximately equivalent to 65–70 lines of poetry), and it is therefore likely that one sheet, which when folded would appear as two pages, was here accidentally omitted from the gathering during the composition of the manuscript.

The manuscript has been dated between 970 and 990 by Robin Flower, who, in an introductory chapter to the facsimile of the *Exeter Book*, provides a full discussion of its date and place of origin, largely from an examination of the script.[1] The scribe was clearly a comparatively reliable copyist, since the emendations required are usually neither extensive nor frequent. Moreover, he cannot even be considered responsible for all the mistakes which do occur, since two distinct types of error are discernible: one depends upon an auditory confusion, e.g. the omission of an elided syllable (Jul. 485) or the spelling *bennum* for *bendum* (Jul. 519); the other depends upon inaccuracy in reading, e.g. mistaking *p* for *þ* (Jul. 294), *ð* for *d*, etc. The latter type of mistake is considerably the more frequent, and it may therefore be conjectured that the scribe of the *Exeter Book* was copying from a manuscript in front of him, which itself already contained errors committed by a scribe who had been working from dictation.

[1] *The Exeter Book of Old English Poetry* (facsimile) 83 ff.

The usual form of punctuation is a dot placed level with the middle of a letter; it is used irregularly, but generally seems to indicate a metrical rather than a grammatical pause. The long poems are divided into sections, which are not, however, marked by Roman numerals as in the Junius and *Beowulf* manuscripts, but by elaborate punctuation marks, the space of a line or half a line, and, usually, an initial capital letter. The sectional divisions in *Juliana* are of 75–85 lines, except for the one beginning on folio 74ᵃ, which has only 32 lines. They do not correspond to major structural points in the narrative, but indicate places at which a pause might suitably be made.

The scribe of the *Exeter Book* used few abbreviations, but these with comparative regularity. They are the common ones: 7 for *ond* (conjunction or first element of compounds); ꝥ for *þæt*, *þoñ* for *þonne*, and the tilde over a preceding vowel to indicate an omitted nasal. Accents in the manuscript appear erratically and infrequently, as may be seen from the complete list in Krapp and Dobbie's edition of the *Exeter Book* (pp. lxxxii ff). There are less than 600 accents altogether, of which 78 occur in *Juliana*. They serve to distinguish homonyms, such as *mán* from *man, mon* (l. 137, etc), and are also placed over monosyllables, such as *æ* (l. 13, etc), and vowels etymologically long. There are, however, a number of short vowels thus marked; sometimes this may be explained as an indication of metrical stress, for example, *ún-* l. 209; a few accents, however, seem quite inexplicable: *má ná* l. 30 (the second accent is almost certainly an error), *ástaʒ* l. 62, etc.

II. Dialect

The dialect of *Juliana*, like that of most extant Old English poetry, is predominantly Late West Saxon, interspersed with a number of Early West Saxon forms and a few Anglianisms. The Late West Saxon forms which are particularly indicative of a late date of transcription are: the unrounding of *y* to *i* in *þince* (l. 87); the spelling of *a* for *o* in the preterite of weak verbs of class II, where the metre requires a secondary stress on this vowel, e.g. *peardade* (l. 20, etc); and the weakening of the vowels

2

of unaccented syllables (particularly when final), such as the appearance of *y* for *i* (Sievers § 142, n.) in *eahtnysse* l. 4, and *-scype* ll. 14 and 208, and of *a* for *e* and vice versa in *þære* (l. 38), *niþa* (l. 203), etc.[1] Although the latter have been regarded as scribal errors by many scholars, who thereby imply that the levelling of vowels in final, unaccented syllables did not begin in the south of England until at least the eleventh century, the number of divergences from correct scribal tradition (76 in the *Exeter Book* alone) cited by Kemp Malone in his article, 'When did Middle English Begin?'[2] strongly suggests that the date of the beginning of levelling should be assigned to the second half of the tenth century.

The most common Early West Saxon features are diphthongization after palatals, to which there are only five exceptions, *eadʒife* 276, etc, *ʒifeð* 388, and *forʒif* 729, and the custom of writing *o* for Germanic *a* before nasals (also found in Anglian), to which there are only eleven exceptions, *ʒelamp* 2, etc.

The chief indications of a non-West Saxon dialect (A) in the phonology and (B) in the grammar are as follows:

(A) (i) occurrence of *e* for WSax *æ* in *pelʒrim* 264 (although this might be a late spelling), and for WSax *ie* in *cpelmdon* 15; (ii) of *æ* for WSax *ie* in *ælde* 727; (iii) of *ē* for WSax *ǣ* in *pēʒe* 487 and *fērblædum* 649, and for WSax *iē* in *preanēd* 464; (iv) absence of broken diphthongs in *paldend* 213, etc, *pideferh* 223, *-ferʒ* 467, and *ʒalʒan* 310, 482; (v) appearance of back mutation in words such as *eodera* 113, *meotud* 182, etc, and with lowering of *io* to *eo* in *speoþum* 188, *leoþu* 592, etc; (vi) the form *syllend* 705 (but *sellend* 668) cf *syllan*, *Beowulf* 2160, 2729, and *sullen* in the ME *Ancrene Wisse*, in all of which the raising of *e* to *y* appears to be the result of a combinative change caused by the *s* reinforced by *l* (Sievers § 124 n. 1, 2); (vii) the form *hildeþremman* 64 (cf *trem*, *Beowulf* 2525), which seems unlikely to be a Kenticism, as this text is not connected to that area by any other form, but cf Wright § 112 n. 1 and § 3 n. 1, where he

---

[1] All editors of *Juliana* have hitherto emended these forms. For a list of similar spellings in *Beowulf* see Klaeber's Introduction in his edition, lxxxi ff.

[2] *Curme Volume of Linguistic Studies*, Baltimore 1930, 110 ff.

maintains that the dialects of E. Sussex and E. Anglia show that the so-called Kentish *e* for *y* was not confined to Kent; cf also the occasional ME lowering of *i* to *e*, e.g. *schemered* (*Sir Gawain* 772), although the usual effect of a nasal is to raise *e* to *i/y*.

(B) (i) use of the originally accentuated forms of the accusative of the personal pronouns, *mec*, *þec*, *usic*, and *eopic*,[1] although both *me* and *þe* each occur three times; (ii) the forms of the weak verbs of class III, *saȝast* 84, *hafast* 96, etc (WSax *sæȝst*, *hæfst*, etc, Sievers § 416 and 417 n. 1c); (iii) unsyncopated forms of the 2nd and 3rd pers.sg. of the present tense, which are here the general rule and required by the metre at ll. 167b, 220b, 371b, 373b, 388b; (iv) weak inflexions of *lufu*, *lufan* 31, etc; (v) pret. pl. of *seon*, *seȝon* 291, and 1st pers.sg.pres. of *beon*, *beom* 438, and the reduplicating pret. of *lacan*, *leolc* 674.

It is generally assumed that the 'signed' poems of Cynewulf were written in Anglian (attempts to place them more precisely in either Northumbria or Mercia have been inconclusive). The chief evidence for this view is the passage of rhyme and assonance in the epilogue to the *Elene* (1236 ff), where imperfect rhymes become true if Anglian forms are substituted for West Saxon. The evidence for an Anglian origin from *Juliana* itself is slight, for not only must many forms such as *paldend* and *meotud* have probably become traditional in poetry, but also most of the Anglianisms could be attributed to scribal variation; whilst the unsyncopated forms of the 2nd and 3rd pers.sg. of the present tense of verbs, although required at some places by the metre, can no longer be considered evidence of Anglian origin in the light of Dr Sisam's arguments (*Studies in the History of Old English Literature* 123–26). The dialect of *Juliana* is in fact remarkable, not for any interesting philological phenomena, but for its unqualified conformity to the 'literary language' of the Late West Saxon poetic manuscripts.

[1] The form *mec*, however, is found on the Alfred Jewel. It is probably an archaism, but might possibly indicate that such forms were still used in EWS.

III. DATE

Despite much discussion and dispute, most early scholars were unanimous in attributing *Juliana* to the eighth century. A reconsideration of the evidence, however, suggests that the *terminus a quo* cannot be much earlier than 800, whilst there is no positive proof that the poem was not written any time up to 900, an approximate limit only then imposed by the comparative regularity of the metre, in contrast, for instance, with *Maldon*, and the presence of Early West Saxon forms probably postulating a transcript made by an Alfredian scribe.

The points which indicate a date for *Juliana* at least some considerable time after *Beowulf* are as follows: (i) the reminiscences in it of the Old English epic, which appear to be the result of deliberate imitation, rather than to be coincidental similarities arising from the borrowing from a common poetic stock [1]; (ii) the rare use of the weak adjective not preceded by the definite article, a phenomenon of which in *Juliana* there is only one example, l. 482 (and that might be an instance of the common confusion between final 'm' and 'n'), whereas in *Beowulf* there are numerous examples; (iii) the absence of words showing contraction, which are proved by the metrical incompleteness of the half-line to have been originally uncontracted, unlike *Beowulf* in which a large number of words require the restoration of uncontracted forms for metrical reasons (see Klaeber, Appendix 3, § 1, and Wrenn 31 ff); (iv) the presence of forms in which distinct syllables are made by vocalic *l*, *r*, *m*, and *n*, to which there is no exception in *Juliana*, whereas in *Beowulf* there are numerous instances where such forms are monosyllabic (see Klaeber, Appendix 3, § 5). The cumulative weight of these points is fairly substantial, although the first two are by no means conclusive, since (i) is based on literary judgement which necessarily introduces a personal element, and (ii) can be explained on the grounds of erratic scribal habits; (iii) and (iv), however, are reasonably sure indications of a date later than *Beowulf*, since, although the argument is based on negative evidence, it is not therefore

[1] A list of the most important resemblances is given on p. 19 below.

suspect, since it would be astonishing if such earlier forms could have disappeared without leaving the slightest trace in the metre. The conclusion which all four points lead to is moreover corroborated by the deductions which may be made from the spelling of Cynewulf's name.

In the four 'signatures' the name is twice spelt *Cynewulf* (*Elene* and *Juliana*), and twice *Cynwulf* (*Crist*, Part II, and the *Fates of the Apostles*), whilst the earlier form of this name was undoubtedly *Cyniwulf* (*Cyni-* is the first element of such names in the *Historia Ecclesiastica* and *Cyniburuh* occurs in the inscription on the Bewcastle Column). The validity of arguments based on the spelling of the name has been doubted by Tupper who pointed out that owing to the difficulties of fitting the rune for ι (*is*) into the acrostic, Cynewulf might well have used an uncommon form of his name.[1] But since the interpretation of the runes at the end of *Juliana* is extremely doubtful, and it may even well be that each group simply represents Cynewulf's name (see section on *Runic Signature*), Tupper's contention should not prevent us from accepting the view that the form with *e* was the usual manner of spelling Cynewulf's name in his own area and time The form *Cynwulf* affords no evidence, as it is not restricted to any period, but is an Anglian variation, since in that dialect words ending in *e* frequently lost their final vowel when compounded: examples of this may be found in the *Liber Vitæ* and in *Beowulf* at l. 1530, where the metre demands that the dissyllabic manuscript form *Hylaces* (probably for earlier *Hyglaces*) be retained.[2]

The first element of such names was first written *Cyne-* in southern charters in about the year 740, and in South Midland documents about 770. Cynewulf must therefore have written after the middle of the eighth century. But in the north the earlier form *Cyni-* survived for a long time: in the *Liber Vitæ* from Lindisfarne, which is at least as late as the beginning of the ninth century, and, if some identifications of persons mentioned therein by name are correct, as late as 830 or 840, there are more than 100 examples of the spelling *Cyni-* and none of

[1] 'The Philological Legend of Cynewulf', PMLA xxvi 241 f.
[2] See Klaeber (ed.), p. lxxxii, and C. L. Wrenn (ed.), n. to l. 1530.

Cyne-. Moreover the so-called *Northumbrian Genealogies* in manuscript Vespasian B.VI, which, as Dr Sisam has shown, probably had their origins in Lichfield in the kingdom of Mercia, show forms with both *e* and *i* around the year 812. If Cynewulf was a Northumbrian, then the very earliest possible date for his work is the beginning of the ninth century, and even if he was a Mercian the supposed *terminus a quo* cannot be shifted back more than one or two decades.[1] It is, however, only necessary to urge that Cynewulf's poetry should be assigned to its earliest possible date, if the poet is assumed to have been a Northumbrian, for it is reasonable to accept the common view that the Danish invasions and occupation largely terminated the scholarship and literary activity of that area. If, however, he was a Mercian, he might well have written at least any time until Alfred's reign, since, as Miss Whitelock has recently reminded us,[2] no lack of a settled culture can be suggested in the area from which Alfred sought scholars to assist him in his plan of educational revival.

The chronology of Cynewulf's known poems cannot be exactly determined. The unusual method of the runic signature suggests that *Juliana* must either have been the first or the last of his extant works, and the comparative lack of ingenuity shown here can be explained either on the grounds of inexperience or exhaustion. The general effect of the poem, however, is that of uninspired competence rather than that of the technical hesitancy of a poet working towards his maturity. It might therefore plausibly be maintained that the *Fates of the Apostles* with its Riddle-like signature was the first of the four Cynewulfian poems, that *Crist* Part II and the *Elene* represent the height of Cynewulf's poetical development, and that *Juliana* shows its decline.

IV. CYNEWULF'S IDENTITY

Three attempts have been made to identify Cynewulf, all of which have been useless because of the frequent occurrence of

[1] The whole of this passage is of course entirely indebted to Dr Sisam's lecture in the *Proceedings of the Brit. Acad.*, xxvii, 303 ff.

[2] 'Anglo-Saxon Poetry and the Historian', *Trans. Royal Hist. Soc.*, 4th series xxxi, p. 81.

the name in documents of the period, and the insufficiency of other evidence. Briefly the suggestions are: (i) Cenulf, Abbot of Peterborough, and later Bishop of Worcester, who died in 1006.[1] This view was early abandoned because the elements of the names, Cen- and Cyn-, are not interchangeable, and the tenth century is undoubtedly too late a date for the poem; (ii) Cynewulf, who was Bishop of Lindisfarne from 737 to 780, a period of political disturbance, and who died in 782.[2] The arguments advanced against this supposition are that the conditions of his time were not favourable to the composition of poetry, that he is nowhere mentioned as a poet, and that his dates are too early; (iii) Cynewulf, a priest, probably in the diocese of Dunwich, who in 803 attended the synod of Clovesho.[3] The evidence for this identification is so slight that it can be neither supported nor refuted.

Equally unprofitable guessing is practised by those who attempt to deduce personal history from the epilogue to the *Elene*, and therefore the negative conclusion is unavoidable that nothing reliable can be said about Cynewulf's identity, character or life history.

V. THE RUNIC SIGNATURE

Cynewulf's naming of himself in the epilogues to *Juliana*, *Elene*, *Crist* II, and *The Fates of the Apostles*, is of remarkable interest from the literary-historical point of view, for it marks the full recognition of a new conception of the poet and the poem in Anglo-Saxon England. It proves the passing of the old anonymous poetry, where no work was held to be any man's personal property, but was handed on with gradual variations and developments, and the acceptance of a new and more sophisticated idea, the belief that it was of importance for the authorship of the poem to be known, and that the poem, once written, was both complete and the possession of the particular poet who composed it. The first traces of this idea are of course

[1] J. M. Kemble, 'On Anglo-Saxon Runes', *Archaeologia* xxviii 362.
[2] F. Dietrich, *Disputatio de Cruce Ruthwellensi* 14, Marburg 1865.
[3] *Crist*, ed. A. S. Cook, Boston, 1900, lxxiii.

easily detectable in Bede's interest in Cædmon's inspiration and knowledge of the words of his first poem. It seems likely in fact that religious poetry, from the earliest time of its composition, was thought to possess a certain sacrosanctity, which conferred dignity on its author and inviolability on itself. But the full development of this idea is historically evident for the first time in Cynewulf's runic device.

The use of colophons was probably traditional; at least in the Latin manuscripts of the period, as Dr Sisam has pointed out,[1] names of authors and scribes are thus preserved in acrostic form, as for instance in Bishop Æpelwald of Lichfield's verses in the *Book of Cerne*, where the name is spelt by the initial capital letters of the lines. This method was of course unsuited to a poetry which was habitually written as prose, and which was primarily intended for recitation (*þe þis ȝied præce*, l. 719). The runes were therefore essential to call attention to the concealed significance of the lines. There may also have been another and less practical reason for their use: the runic alphabet had ancient magical associations—there is a famous description, for instance, of its supernatural origin and magical powers in the Old Norse *Hávámal*—and traces of these associations undoubtedly survived into the Christian period, as the use of runes in the Charm *Þiþ Lenctenadle* testifies; it is therefore quite possible that Cynewulf inherited a superstitious belief in the efficacy of the futhorc, and so contrived to write his name in runes, not only as a convenient method of commemorating himself, but also supposing it to be in itself an auspicious action.

Cynewulf's use of runes in *Juliana* differs from that in the other 'signed' poems, for in them each rune is separate and its name forms part of the sentence, whilst in *Juliana* the runes are arranged in groups; whether each group is equivalent to a word, or whether each is equivalent to the name Cynewulf, has remained in dispute. The investigation of this runic signature is heavily impeded by lack of evidence, and unfortunately no theory can be considered conclusive. The interpretation of Trautmann, [2] the chief exponent of the first view stated above,

---

[1] *op.cit.* 321.
[2] *Kynewulf der Bischof und Dichter*, BBA I 47.

that ᚻ·ᚱ·ᚣ· should be taken as *cyn*, ᛗ·ᛈ·ᚾ as *epu*, a Northumbrian variant of West Saxon *eopan*, and ·ᛁ·ᚠ· as *licfæt*, has been argued by Dr Sisam to be strained and improbable,[1] whilst Mr R. W. V. Elliott has recently made a fresh and valuable defence of the older view.[2] The crucial point at issue lies in the word *epu*, since both the first and the last rune group may be given a meaning without too much difficulty. Mr Elliott claims that *epu* could have the generic sense 'sheep', citing in support of this contention the Gothic *awepi* 'flock of sheep', and the one recorded example in Bosworth-Toller of *epes* (gen.sg.) : *ovis*. Now since ultimately both *epu* and *ovis* derive from the same root, it is reasonable to suppose that *epu* did not originally have its later limited sense, and in fact its general sense survived in the precise cognate to the Gothic word, Old English *eopde*: this, however, does not throw any light on how Old English *epu* was used. Nor does Mr Elliott's instance of *epe* : *ovis* serve his argument, for here the form of the word is masculine, the feminine grammatical gender, apparently for the sake of clarity of distinction, being discarded in favour of natural gender. There is therefore no evidence whatsoever that *epu* (fem.), as opposed to *epe* (masc.), could have any meaning in Old English but 'female sheep'; that the force of this meaning was clearly retained is shown by quotations in Bosworth-Toller where it is either placed in contrast to *ramm* or as a subdivision of the general term *sceap*. At best then that *epu* could mean sheep is a guess, but so also is Dr Sisam's view that the poet's full name should be understood in each of the rune groups, since there is no other example of this practice. According to the facts which we possess then, either Cynewulf made what was at very least an unhappy use of the word *epu*, allowing the lines containing his name to be more weak and obscure than he did elsewhere,[3] or he used the runes in a manner which is unique in extant literature. The poet's usage

[1] *op.cit.* 318.

[2] 'Cynewulf's Runes in *Juliana* and *Fates of the Apostles*', *English Studies* xxxiv, 193 ff. Cf also *M.L.N.* lxxii, 538.

[3] It is worth noticing that this was not the only method of dividing his name into rune groups open to Cynewulf. Spelt 'Cynwulf', the name falls

in his other three 'signed' poems provides plausible a priori grounds for seeking some meaning other than the name Cynewulf in the three runic groups at the end of *Juliana*, but whether this process of argument by analogy is useful here, or whether it is misleading, must remain open to doubt.

VI. The Legend

The martyrdom of Juliana took place during the Diocletian persecution, and was probably first set down in writing in the reign of Constantine, when the Church, at last unmolested, zealously sought out the names and histories of her martyrs. But of many there remained only some brief entry in a martyrology: men of pious intention, therefore, expanded these as seemed fitting to them with accounts of miracles and tortures derived either from the New Testament or from some of the other more authentic records of the Church.

Of such a kind is probably the earliest extant life of Juliana, printed in the *Acta Sanctorum* of Bolland,[1] under the heading, *Acta auctore anonymo ex xi veteribus MSS*, in the form of a critical text based on these eleven manuscripts.[2] The original date of this life cannot be given with any exactitude, but in that the translation of the saint's body from Pozzuoli, where it had been taken by Sophia,[3] to Cumæ,[4] is not mentioned, it is assumed that it was written earlier than the second half of the sixth century, during which period, according to Petrus Subdiaconus, this event took place, *imminente Ethnica feritate*, which Bolland interprets as a reference to the invasion of Italy by the Lombards in 568.

easily into two elements, which, in view of the possibility of using *wulf* of the devil (cf *Riddles* ed. Tupper, n. to Riddle 90), could have been embodied without much difficulty into 'a sentence referring to the Last Judgement.

[1] *Acta Sanctorum, Februarius* II, 873 ff.

[2] Another text of the *Vita* and two shorter versions are printed by Brunöhler from MSS in Munich.

[3] *op.cit.* 877.

[4] 'Alia Vita', *Acta Sanctorum, Feb. II*, 882.

JULIANA

Besides this life, there were, before Cynewulf's time, references to Juliana in martyrologies, the earliest of which is the so-called *Martyrologium Vetustissimum*, ascribed to St Jerome (d. 420), where under the date xiv *kal. Mart.* there is this entry: 'Nicomedia, passio S. Julianæ virginis, et Martyris'.[1] Similar entries occur in other Latin martyrologies printed in Migne's *Patrologia Latina*. Of more relevance, however, is the following passage from Bede's *Martyrology*:

> Et in Cumis natale sanctæ Julianæ virginis, quæ tempore Maximiani imperatoris primo a suo patre Africano cæsa, et graviter cruciata, deinde et a præfecto Eleusio, quem sponsum habuerat, nuda virgis cæsa, et a capillis suspensa est, et plumbo soluto capite perfusa, et rursum in carcerem recepta, ubi palam cum diabolo conflixit, et rursus evocata rotarum tormenta, flammas ignium, ollam ferventem superavit, ac decollatione capitis martyrium consummavit. Quæ passa est quidem in Nicomedia, sed post paucum tempus Deo disponente in Campaniam translata.[2]

This suggests that by the eighth century there was in England a full-length life of Juliana, from which this epitome was made. It is at any rate evident from Aldhelm's *de laudibus Virginitatis* that already around the year 700 legends of miracles and martyrdoms in distant parts of Asia were both popular and current in England.

Many versions of the legend were composed after Cynewulf's period,[3] of which the most important before the Middle Ages are the Μαρτύριον τῆς ʽαγίας μαρτύρος ʼIουλιανῆς τῆς ἐν Nικομηδίᾳ of Simeon Metaphrastes, printed in Migne[4] with a sixteenth-century Latin translation (*Latine apud Surium ad diem 16 Februarii*),[5] and the Latin life by Petrus Subdiaconus, written about 1100, and printed by Bolland under the title *Alia Vita*.[6] During the Middle Ages up to the year 1484, when, in the *Legenda Aurea*, there appeared the first printed account of Juliana, numerous English lives of the saint were composed, amongst

---

[1] *Patrologia Latina* 30, col. 444.   [2] *op.cit.* 94, colls. 843 f.
[3] A full list is given in Professor d'Ardenne's edition of the ME life, Introduction § 2.
[4] *Patrologia Graeca* 114, colls. 1437 ff.
[5] Translated by Lippoman, and incorporated in Surius' *Lives of the Saints.*   [6] *Vita, op.cit.* 878.

which is the Early Middle English life, which survives in MS Bodley 34 and MS Royal 17 A, xxvii, and which has been edited by Professor d'Ardenne.

The main facts of Juliana's life according to the Latin and Greek authors are briefly as follows: she was the daughter of Affricanus of Nicomedia, who betrothed her in her ninth year,[1] to Eleusius, a senator and friend of Galerius Maximian. When she reached the age of eighteen,[2] Eleusius became anxious that the wedding should take place. But Juliana, though a pagan by birth, had become a convert to Christianity, and therefore refused to marry Eleusius, unless he too accepted the Christian faith. In order to break her resolve, Eleusius commanded her to be tortured and then cast into prison, where the devil appeared to her. Finally, after miraculously escaping from various other torments, she was beheaded, thus dying a martyr's death. Shortly afterwards Sophia (Sophronia), a woman of senatorial rank, who happened to be passing through Nicomedia to Rome, took the saint's body, and, being driven by storms to Campania, placed it in the mausoleum at Pozzuoli,[3] from where in the second half of the sixth century it was transferred to Cumæ; in 1207, however, the relics were once more removed, and deposited in the Convent of S. Maria de Donna Aromata at Naples.[4] There is much controversy over their subsequent history, and today many European churches are said to possess certain portions of them, one of the most famous being the Church of Notre Dame des Victoires du Sablon in Brussels.[5]

It is possible that the text printed in Bolland, and generally referred to as the *Vita* or *Acta*, is not the exact version used by Cynewulf,[6] although the general similarity in the progress of the action, and many sentences of identical phraseology, suggest that Cynewulf's original was closely related to it. The only evidence, which indicates that the *Vita* may at least not have been Cynewulf's sole source, is the inconsistency between

---

[1] Metaphrastes in *Patrologia Graeca* 114, col. 1451.

[2] Metaphrastes, *op.cit.* col. 1451.   [3] *Vita, op.cit.* 877.

[4] 'Translatio III S. Julianæ', *Acta Sanctorum, Februarius* II 882 ff.

[5] d'Ardenne, *op.cit.* 18.

[6] The gaps in the manuscript increase the difficulty of determining this, cf notes to ll. 288 and 588.

ll. 28 ff and ll. 46 ff which reflect two distinct conceptions of Juliana's motive. According to the first she is, like St Agnes for instance, one of the *devotæ* who, in accordance with the Church's exaltation of virginity, renounced the idea of marriage to lead a life dedicated to God, though not, as later, out of their parents' home. The second explanation, however, is simply that she will not submit to marriage with a heathen, for *cultus disparitas* was already regarded as an impediment to marriage by the Fathers, who had as their Biblical authority 1 Cor. vii, 39 ('cui vult nubat: tantum in Domino'). This inconsistency would be conclusive proof that Cynewulf had before him either two versions of the legend, or one, which could not be the *Vita*, were it not for the possibility that the motive stated at ll. 28 ff was Cynewulf's own addition, invented for the immediate effect of increasing Juliana's piety and religious devotion, but without regard to perfect consistency. The exaltation of virginity was of course as familiar to Anglo-Saxon as to Latin writers (the influence of hagiography containing this motif can be seen in *Judith*, for instance), and it is therefore hypothetically as probable that this addition to the Juliana legend sprang from Cynewulf as from a Latin writer. It should be noticed, however, that the *Vita*, which never states the first motive, nevertheless points the virtue of virginity, when the devil exclaims to Juliana, 'O virginitas, quid contra nos armaris.' Moreover, Juliana's concern for her virginity is also emphasized in the *Liflade* and in an Old French version (described by d'Ardenne pp. xx f). In the former Juliana's demand that Eleusius should obtain a higher rank before she will consent to marry him is represented as a deliberate stratagem, designed to enable her to evade the marriage, and therefore her second condition had presumably the same intention. The unreasonableness of the *Vita* and the inconsistency of Cynewulf's poem are thus both avoided, and it may well be thought that the *Liflade* here shows us the original form of the story. In this case Cynewulf's version, with its omission of Juliana's first demand[1] and

---

[1] Juliana's condition that Eleusius should obtain the prefecture is also, according to Schaar, missing from the Middle High German and Scottish versions of the legend.

emphasis on virginity, would show a confused handling of such
a source, but whether the confusion was Cynewulf's own, or
that of an intermediary text, would still remain open to doubt.

The most interesting and significant difference between the
two works, however, lies in the treatment of the character of
Eleusius. In accordance with the typical Anglo-Saxon preference for villains to be utterly bad, Cynewulf has considerably
blackened the prefect's behaviour. In the *Vita*, Eleusius appears
as an easy-going man, eager to marry Juliana, and willing to
please her even to the extent of theoretically accepting Christianity: in fact, only refusing to be baptized for fear of the
Emperor depriving him of both office and life. He only attempts
to impose his wishes on Juliana by torture when she refuses his
offered compromise. In Cynewulf's version, however, the issue
is much more clear cut. Eleusius's casual tolerance has been
replaced by a zeal in the service of the heathen, devil-inspired
idols, which is almost as keen as Juliana's devotion to Christianity, and he thus demands from the outset her acquiescence
and submission to his gods. The struggle then is clearly between
good and evil, and Eleusius is made as deliberately wicked as
Juliana is good. By this means a greater sense of ultimate
importance is gained, whilst ordinary psychological probability
is lost.[1]

Whilst Cynewulf's most striking departure from his source
is in his treatment of the character of Eleusius, other modi-
fications may be seen in the structure and in the smaller details
of his work. In order to give *Juliana* a dramatic shape and
texture not possessed by the *Vita*, Cynewulf modulated his
emphases, so that the story, instead of progressing as a sequence
of events, unrelieved by dramatic emphasis, has acquired a
more closely knit and more effective structure, notably by
Cynewulf's pointing of the scene between Juliana and the devil,
which thus becomes the dramatic core of the work. This in-
tensification of interest in Juliana's spiritual combat with the
devil owes its relevance, of course, to the portraying of Eleusius
as the servant of the devil, who assists him in his attempted

---

[1] The same approach is seen in *Judith* in the treatment of the character of Holofernes.

15

conquest of Juliana. Thus the alterations in characterization and structure are carefully interwoven.

Cynewulf also gave his story shape by pruning away some of the excessive detail of his original, particularly facts which would seem irrelevant to an Anglo-Saxon audience. Thus he gives none of the *Vita's* account of the translation and burial of the saint's body, but implies briefly that her funeral took place in Nicomedia. Cynewulf also omits points in the *Vita*, which to an Anglo-Saxon might seem discordant in tone. Where the Latin Juliana, for instance, flings the devil, despite his appeal for mercy, *in locum stercore plenum*, the Anglo-Saxon Juliana sets him free; and where the *Vita's* final description of the fate of Eleusius and his followers is 'ab avibus et feris corpora eorum sunt devorata', Cynewulf's grim conclusion is of a typically Anglo-Saxon kind.

A small point of interest is the absence in *Juliana* of the names of the Latin gods; but there is no need to deduce from this with Backhaus [1] and Fritzche,[2] that they were deliberately suppressed by the poet, for fear that the mere mention of the names of heathen gods, who had never been worshipped in England, might disturb the yet unstable faith of his readers, although they and their forefathers had been Christian for about 200 years; nor to suppose with Strunk [3] that it seemed dangerous to Cynewulf to mention the names of what he still believed to be hostile, supernatural powers. The explanation is probably far more simple and practical: it is, that the fitting of Latin names into Old English metre was extremely difficult, and often resulted in a weak half-line, and Cynewulf therefore avoided them as often as possible; Affricanus, for instance, is only mentioned once by name, and Eleusius three times.[4]

[1] *Über die Quelle der mittelenglischen Legende von der heiligen Juliana*, Halle 1899, 25.

[2] 'Das angelsächsische Gedicht Andreas und Cynewulf', *Anglia* II 459.

[3] Introduction xxiv.

[4] Another instance of this is at l. 304, where a reference to the Crucifixion is inserted between references to the martyrdoms of St Peter and St Andrew, instead of forming, as one might have expected, the climax of the narration of the devil's wickedness. The explanation is surely that few words in Anglo-Saxon begin in 'p', but the *Pilatus* conveniently

The numerous verbal echoes of the *Vita* in *Juliana* makes it seem probable that Cynewulf was following a Latin source, either identical with, or at least very similar to the text printed by Bolland. The many deviations, however, which clearly bear an Anglo-Saxon stamp, show that Cynewulf by no means followed it uncritically, but rather impressed his own conception upon it, and gave it a dramatic form, which belies the usual modern criticism that Anglo-Saxon poets lacked a sense of form. Cynewulf's treatment of the legend in fact shows all the confidence and the poise of a skilful poet working in an established tradition.

VII. THE STYLE

Apart from certain stylized passages, such as the opening section, the diction and syntax of *Juliana* are more nearly those of prose than in any other Old English poem of this type. Its style has been called 'classic' by Dr Sisam, in the sense that the prose of Ælfric is classic as compared with that of Alfred. Whilst it would be a rash exaggeration to press the parallel too far, for Cynewulf still retains a few of the ancient poetic compounds and a few of the repetitionary variations, yet it may be said that the style of *Juliana* and of Ælfric's *Lives of the Saints* have some important qualities in common: clarity and directness, simplicity and smoothness. *Juliana*, however, has the defect of these virtues, a uniformity verging on monotony. The style—the word is being used in its broadest sense—is generally unrelieved by any emotional or rhetorical emphasis or by any other gradations in tone. Interesting exceptions to this are at ll. 93 ff and ll. 166 ff which echo a Latin warmth; the first passage, however, is derived straight from the *Vita*, though the second is apparently expanded from the barer *dulcissima mea Juliana* of the original. But these, whilst pleasant in themselves, fit somewhat incongruously into the bleaker atmosphere

alliterates with *Petrus and Paulus*. In the *Vita* the devil's evil-doing is related in roughly chronological order, and in the reference to the Crucifixion it is Judas who is mentioned, not Pilate.

of the northern poem, and the true native vigour, found occasionally, as at ll. 216 ff, is preferable.

Such variations in tone, however, are unfortunately incidental, as is the imagery. The kenning and the imaginative poetic compound were clearly by the date of *Juliana* extinct, except in so far as a few remained (e.g. *spanrad*) as a fossilized part of the poetic language, whilst the resulting bareness was hardly broken by the use of simile or metaphor. In *Juliana*, nevertheless, there are two striking images: one at ll. 595 ff, which, though it may seem trite today when the comparison has almost passed into common speech, was presumably not hackneyed and outworn in Cynewulf's time; and the other at ll. 400 ff, of the human mind and body as a fortress, defending itself against the onslaughts of the devil, which appears to contain, as it were in a nutshell, the basic allegory of Mediaeval Morality plays.[1]

The common habit of interpreting Christian characters and situations in terms of heroic society is preserved in *Juliana*, though to a less extent than in such a poem as the *Andreas*. Peter and Paul are called *Cristes þeᵹnas*, Eleusius *æþelinᵹ, hererinc, hildepremma*, etc, whilst the variations of God include *æþelinᵹa pyn* and *beorna hleo*.[2] The fullest account of heroic custom, however, is at ll. 683 ff, where the poet adds to his statement that Heliseus and his followers were drowned and went to hell the curious comment that there, on the benches of the winehall, the men had no need to look for gold from their lord: a typical example of Old English litotes, but one which

---

[1] Schaar in *Critical Studies in the Cynewulf Group* 30 suggests that the source for both the image at ll. 382 ff and this one is St Jerome's *Comment. in Ep. ad Ephesios*, bk III, ch. vi. The phrase *ᵹuðlic ᵹuðreaf*, however, suggests a definite reminiscence of Ephesians vi, 16, and similar references to the Pauline 'armour of God', whether direct or at second hand, occur in *Beowulf* 1724 ff and *Crist* 681 ff. For the commonness of this image in Anglo-Saxon sermons, cf Whitelock, *The Audience of Beowulf* 8. Since there is therefore no reason to suppose that the first part of this passage was borrowed from St Jerome, it is the less likely that the second was. It appears at any rate to be unique in vernacular literature until the Middle Ages.

[2] A list of synonyms for warrior, enemy, sea, etc, common in heroic poetry and also found in the works of the Cynewulfian 'school' is provided by Schaar 390 ff.

produces here a grimly incongruous effect.[1] Whether the use of such heroic details in *Juliana* sprang from a conscious attempt to glorify the Christian story, and to show that the founders and the upholders of the new religion were in no way inferior to Germanic heroes, or from the mere observance of convention, remains open to doubt. The same is true of the reminiscences of *Beowulf*, although their number and their use (e.g. the introduction of the devil by *þa cpom semninʒa*) suggest that Cynewulf deliberately intended to recall *Beowulf* and thus to impart an epic quality to his narrative. The following are the most important parallels [2]: 27 *hine fyrpet bræc*, 232 etc; 168 *ʒinfæste ʒiefe*, 1271; 242 *ða cpom semninʒa*, 710; 246 *helle hæftlinʒ*, 788; 253 *pes þu on ofeste*, 386; 359 *anes cræfte*, 699; 418 *earmsceapen*, 1351; 429 *perʒa*, 133, 1747; 430 *earm aʒlæca*, 592; 457 *helle ʒæst*, 1274; 464 *preaned polian*, 284; 474 f *him lasta pearð siðast ʒesyne*, 1402 f; 486 *beore druncne*, 480; 567 *heoroʒiferne*, 1498; 601 *eafoða ʒemyndiʒ*, 1530; 615 *hearmleoð agol*, 786.

But the sparse imagery and the conventional heroic terms are only minor adornments to a poem in which emotional overtones and stylistic variations are reduced to a minimum. *Juliana* clearly comes at the end of a period. Though it parades remnants of the old heroic style, the spirit and general effect are different. There could be no poetic progress from it: beyond lie monotony or prose. Competent in itself, though lacking the poetic mastery of the *Elene* or *Crist*, *Juliana* brings Old English poetry into a blind alley. Whether the other 'signed' poems represent Cynewulf's efforts to retrace his steps, or whether *Juliana* was literally the end of his poetic career, remains in a sense an academic question. But all the other Cynewulfian poetry is but a temporary postponement of a natural conclusion reached in *Juliana*. Thus whilst it is a mistake to regard the poem as scholars have done hitherto, as merely of philological and antiquarian interest, it cannot be denied that its smooth competence is achieved at the expense of a certain thinness and lack of vigour and variety.

[1] The only other description of hell in the terms of the meadhall is in *Genesis B* 410 ff, where it also has an ironic force.

[2] The line reference given first is that of *Juliana*, that after the quotation refers to *Beowulf*.

A NOTE ON THE TEXT AND TEXTUAL NOTES

The text of the present edition was transcribed from the facsimile of
the *Exeter Book*, and afterwards checked against the manuscript. The
punctuation, use of capitals, and paragraphing are as far as possible in
accordance with modern usage; all the MS abbreviations (see Introd. 2),
with the exception of 7 for *ond*, have been expanded, without comment.
Emendations adopted in the text are followed in the list of variants by
'Ed' if common, and otherwise by a reference to their originator. Justi-
fication of new emendations will be found in the notes. All references in
the notes to other OE poems are to the *Anglo-Saxon Poetic Records* series.

JULIANA

(*Exeter Book, fols. 65ᵇ-76ᵃ*)

Hpæt! Þe ðæt hyrdon   hæleð eahtian,
deman dædhpate,   þætte in daȝum ȝelamp
Maximianes,   se ȝeond middanȝeard,
arleas cyning,   eahtnysse ahof,
5 cpealde Cristne men,   circan fylde,
ȝeat on ȝræspong   Ɉodherȝendra,
hæþen hildfruma,   haliȝra blod,
ryhtfremmendra.   Þæs his rice brad,
pid 7 peorðlic   ofer perþeode,
10 lytesna ofer ealne   yrmenne ȝrund.
Foron æfter burȝum,   spa he biboden hæfde,
þegnas þryðfulle;   oft hi þræce rærdon,
dædum ȝedpolene,   þa þe Dryhtnes æ
feodon þurh firencræft;   feondscype rærdon,
15 hofon hæþenȝield,   halge cpelmdon,
breotun boccræftȝe,   bærndon ȝecorene,
ȝæston Ɉodes cempan   ȝare 7 liȝe.
    Sum pæs æhtpelig   æþeles cynnes,
rice ȝerefa;   rondburȝum peold,
20 eard peardade   oftast symle

TEXTUAL VARIANTS: (6) *ȝodherȝendra* Ed, MS *ȝod herȝenda*. (12) *oft* Ed,
MS *of*. (16) *bærndon* Ed, MS *bærdon*.

---

(4) *eahtnysse*. Although the MS form with *ea* cannot be a phonological
development from the historical *e*, it occurs too frequently to be regarded
as a scribal vagary. It is probably a late spelling caused by the coinciding
in pronunciation of *e* and *ea* as [æ].

(16) *breotun*. cp *abreot, Beowulf* 2930, and *abreoton, Andreas* 51. The
confusion may first have arisen through the Northumbrian interchange
of *ēa* and *ēo*, whereupon in this word an infinitive *breatan* might well be
given the parts of a reduplicating verb on the model of *beatan*.

(20) *oftast symle*. Trautmann proposed emending *oftast* to *onpist* on the
grounds that the phrase as it stands is a contradiction in terms. But in
the Lindisfarne Matthew ix, 14, the Latin *frequenter* is glossed *oft 7 symle*
(Rushworth has *ȝelome*). This type of phrase may therefore be assumed
to be idiomatic, *symle* having lost the full force of its independent
meaning.

21

JULIANA

in þære ceastre Commedia,
heold hordʒestreon. Oft he hæþenʒield,
ofer pord Ʒodes, peoh ʒesohte
neode ʒeneahhe. Þæs him noma cenned
25 Heliseus, hæfde ealdordom
micelne 7 mærne. Ða his mod ongon
fæmnan lufian, (hine fyrpet bræc),
Iulianan. Hio in ʒæste bær
halʒe treope, hoʒde ʒeorne
30 þæt hire mæʒ̆had mana ʒehpylces
fore Cristes lufan clæne ʒeheolde.
    Ða pæs sio fæmne, mid hyre fæder pillan,
peleʒum bipeddad; pyrd ne ful cuþe,
freondrædenne hu heo from hoʒde,
35 ʒeonʒ on ʒæste. Hire pæs Ʒodes eʒsa
mara in ʒemyndum þonne eall þæt maþþumʒesteald
þe in þæs æþelinʒes æhtum punade.
Þa pæs se peliʒa þære pifʒifta,
ʒoldspediʒ ʒuma, ʒeorn on mode,
40 þæt him mon fromlicast fæmnan ʒeʒyrede,
bryd to bolde. Heo þæs beorn s lufan
fæste piðhoʒde, þeah þe feohʒestreon
under hordlocan, hyrsta unrim,
æhte ofer eorþan Heo þæt eal forseah,
45 7 þæt pord acpæð on pera menʒu:
"Ic þe mæʒ ʒesecʒan þæt þu þec sylfne ne þearft

(46) *ic* Ed, MS *in*.

---

(38) *þære pifʒifta*. *Pifʒifta* only occurs in the plural, presumably
influenced by the Latin *nuptiæ*, which it in fact renders in this context.
It is distinct from the sg *ʒifte* 'dowry'. For the form *þære* cf Introduction 3.

(42) *þeah þe*. A pronominal subject need not be inserted here, nor in
ll. 103 and 219. For similar omissions after *þeah þe* and *forþon* see A.
Pogatscher, 'Unausgedrücktes Subjekt im Altenglischen', *Anglia* xxiii,
p. 274.

(44) *æhte*. This is an old optative form showing *i*-mutation. Similar
examples, where the vowel of the indicative has not been introduced
into the subjunctive, occur in other preterite-present verbs, e.g. *dyʒe*
(Wright § 482).

22

spiþor spencan;   ʒif þu soðne Ʒod
lufast 7 ʒelyfest,   7 his lof rærest,
onʒietest ʒæsta Hleo,   ic beo ʒearo sona
50 unpaclice   pillan þines.
Spylce ic þe secʒe,   ʒif þu to sæmran ʒode
þurh deofolʒield   dæde biþencest,
hætsð hæþenfeoh,   ne meaht þu habban mec,
ne ʒeþreatian   þe to sinhiʒan;
55 næfre þu þæs spiðlic   sar ʒeʒearpast,
þurh hæstne nið,   heardra pita,
þæt þu mec onpende   porda þissa."
     Ða se æþelinʒ pearð   yrre ʒebolʒen,
firendædum fah,   ʒehyrde þære fæmnan pord;
60 het ða ʒefetiʒan   ferend snelle,
hreoh 7 hyʒeblind,   haliʒre fæder
recene to rune.   Reord up astaʒ,
siþþan hy toʒædre   ʒaras hlændon,

---

(53) *hæþenfeoh* Strunk, MS *hæþen peoh*. (54) *sinhiʒan*, MS *ʒe sinʒan*.

---

(53) *hætsð. sð* for *st* (inflexion of indic.pres.2sg.) is a feature of EWS and is particularly common in the Hatton MS of the *Cura Pastoralis*.

(53) *hæþenfeoh* (MS *hæþenpeoh*). Despite some slight support for the MS reading from *Beowulf* 175 f, the emendation is required here, since the rendering *hatan* 'dedicate' is unlikely, there being no recorded instance of this usage or of any sense related to it. For the meaning 'vow' cf *ða ðing þe he ðær to gode hett* (*Cura Pastoralis* [Alfred's version] ed. Sweet 84, l. 17), and *ece hett*, which glosses *æterna promisit* (Lindisfarne Luke ix, 2). Thorpe (apparently by mistake) also reads *-feoh*.

(54) *sinhiʒan* (MS *ʒesinʒan*). The scribe evidently had difficulty with this word: the form here is very dubious, as the syllable *hī* could hardly have been syncopated, and at l. 698, where the medial syllable is required by the metre, the reading is *sinhpan*, with an *i* inserted above the line. The restoration of the usual form here, though necessary, results in an improbable metrical type, unless the prefix *ʒe* is omitted. The latter would not be a startling omission, since *ʒe* is used so frequently and erratically, that only those instances of it, where it is required by sense or metre, can be safely attributed to the author. Here the prefix may well have been added by analogy with *ʒeþreatian* in the first half-line. The alternate (unpublished) suggestion of Professor Wrenn, that *ʒesin-ʒan* is here a nonce word, a noun derived from *synʒian* 'to sin', the *ʒe* implying fellowship, is pleasing, but does not account for the similar error at l. 698, and does not provide such a suitable object to *habban*.

hildeþremman.   Hæðne pæron beȝen
65 synnum seoce,   speor 7 aþum.
Ða reordode   rices hyrde
piðþære fæmnan fæder   frecne mode,
daraðhæbbende: "Me þin dohtor hafað
ȝeyped orpyrðu;   heo me on an saȝað
70 þæt heo mæȝlufan   minre ne ȝyme,
freondrædenne.   Me þa fraceðu sind
on modsefan   mæste peorce,
þæt heo mec spa torne   tæle ȝerahte
fore þissum folce;   het me fremdne ȝod,
75 ofer þa oþre   þe pe ær cuþon,
pelum peorþian,   pordum lofian,
on hyȝe herȝan,   oþþe hi nabban."
    Ȝespearc þa spiðferð   speor æfter porde,
þære fæmnan fæder,   ferðlocan ònspeon:
80 "Ic þæt ȝesperȝe   þurh soð ȝodu,
spa ic are æt him   æfre finde,
oþþe, þeoden, æt þe   þine hyldu
pinburȝum in,   ȝif þas pord sind soþ,
monna leofast,   þe þu me saȝast,
85 þæt ic hy ne spariȝe,   ac on spild ȝiefe,
þeoden mæra,   þe to ȝepealde.
Dem þu hi to deaþe,   ȝif þe ȝedafen þince,
spa to life læt,   spa þe leofre sy."
    Eode þa fromlice   fæmnan to spræce,

(64) *pæron, pær* in a different hand and ink over an erasure. (72) *mod-sefan*, upper part of *e* erased so that it resembles an 'ı'. (74) *fremdne*, *n* written over an erasure. (78) *speor* Ed (except Gollancz), MS *spor*. (86) *ȝepealde* Ed (except Grein), MS *ȝe peald*. (88) *spaþer*, MS *spa*.

---

(71) *freondrædenne* (and l. 34): GK *amor conjugalis*; a rare usage but cf. *freondmynd* and MED s.v. *frend* 3 and NED s.v. *friend* 4.
(78) *speor* (MS *spor*). The MS reading results in an awkward construction, *spor æfter porde...ic þæt ȝesperȝe*. For *speor* cf l. 65.
(79) *ferðlocan onspeon*: 'he spoke', literally 'he opened the chest of his thoughts'. Cf l. 234, *Elene* 86, *Crist* 1055, *Wanderer* 13–14, etc. When not combined with verbs of opening or closing such compounds retain only the meaning of the first element, e.g. *Andreas* 1570.

90 anræd 7 yfelþþeorჳ,   yrre ჳebolჳen,
   þær he ჳlædmode   ჳeonჳe þiste
   þic þeardian.   He þa þorde cþæð:
   "Ðu eart dohtor min   seo dyreste
   7 seo speteste   in sefan minum,
95 anჳe for eorþan,   minra eaჳna leoht,
   Iuliana!   þu on ჳeaþe hafast,
   þurh þin orleჳu,   unbiþyrfe
   ofer þitena dom   þisan ჳefonჳen;
   þiðsæcest þu to spiþe   sylfre rædes
100 þinum brydჳuman,   se is betra þonne þu,
   æþelra for eorþan,   æhtspediჳra
   feohჳestreona;   he is to freonde ჳod.
   Forþon is þæs þyrþe,   þæt þu þæs þeres friჳe,
   ece eadlufan,   an ne forlæte."

(90) *yfel-*, MS *yre*.   (91) *ჳlædmode* Cosijn, MS *ჳlæd mod*.

---

(90) *yreþþeorჳ*. The first element cannot be a mistake for *yrre* since this word occurs in the second half-line. As it stands, *yre-* either equals 'axe-head' or the rune-name 'bow'. Neither of these gives good sense, and anyway, like Ettmüller's suggestion of *irenþþeorჳ*, is improbable in that this type of compound containing a metaphorical comparison is scarcely ever found in OE (cf Appendix s.v. *sunsciene*). Other proposed emendations are Trautmann's *ofer-* and *inþþeorჳ*, the latter possible because of analogous epithets such as *infrod*, etc, and because the error would be palaeographically plausible. Holthausen's view that *þþeorჳ* alone should be read is also possible in that *þþeorჳ* is nowhere else compounded, and that *yre-* could be an error of dittography. The best solution, however, is perhaps to assume an original reading of *yfelþþeorჳ*, a satisfactory compound: the mistake might then have arisen through a confusion over the runic letter *yr*, written probably in Cynewulf's autograph. That this rune in the other three 'signed' poems has the meaning *yfel* has been strongly argued by Trautmann (BBA xxvii, p. 137), and by Gollancz (Cynewulf's *Crist* 117 f), and tentatively accepted by Krapp.

(91) *ჳlædmode* (MS *ჳlæd mod*). In support of the MS reading BT cite: *affrican hire feader feng on earst feire on to lokin ჳef he mahte wið eani luue speden* (*Seinte Juliene* 94 ff). But here this meaning would be rather strained, and anyway the metre requires the emendation.

(104) *an ne forlæte*. 'Leave alone', i.e. 'neglect, forsake'. *An* is a prepositional adverb often combined with *forlætan* to form a quasi-compound. An intervening *ne* occurs also in *Andreas* 1434. In *Daniel* 19 and Crist 1453 *an* is inflected to agree with the object of *forlætan*. Cf *Daniel* 309.

25

105 Him þa seo eadȝe aȝeaf ondspare,
    Iuliana (hio to Ȝode hæfde
    freondrædenne fæste ȝestaþelad):
    "Næfre ic þæs þeodnes þafian wille
    mæȝrædenne, nemne he mæȝna Ȝod
110 ȝeornor b˙ȝonȝe þonne he ȝen dyde,
    lufiȝe mid lacum þone þe leoht ȝescop,
    heofon 7 eorðan 7 holma biȝonȝ,
    eodera ymbhpyrft. Ne mæȝ he elles mec
    brinȝan to bolde. He þa brydlufan
115 sceal to oþerre æhtȝestealdum
    idese secan; nafað he æniȝe her."
        Hyre þa þurh yrre aȝeaf ondspare
    fæder feondlice, nales frætpe onheht:
    "Ic þæt ȝefremme, ȝif min feorh leofað,
120 ȝif þu unrædes ær ne ȝespicest,
    7 þu fremdu ȝodu forð biȝonȝest,
    7 þa forlætest þe us leofran sind,
    þe þissum folce to freme stondað,
    þæt þu unȝeara ealdre scyldiȝ
125 þurh deora ȝripe deaþe speltest,

(116) *æniȝe* Ettmüller, MS *æniȝ*.

---

(116) *æniȝe* (MS *æniȝ*). The emendation *æniȝe* is preferable to *ænȝe* since it makes the scribal error more understandable. Although only a small number of such unsyncopated forms occur in the *Exeter Book*, those enumerated by von der Warth are sufficient to prove their genuineness, and Sievers' objection that these medial vowels are not metrically valid (*Altgermanische Metrik* § 76, 1) is hardly tenable.

(124) *ealdre*. There are eight recorded instances of the construing of *scyldiȝ* with the dative instead of the genitive. Here and at *Daniel* 449 it might be the result of the slurring together in dictation of the final and initial 's', a common type of error, e.g. *Renaude saule* (*Sir Gawain* 1916). In two other examples the use of the dative might have been caused by analogy with the Latin: *spa moneȝum scyldum scyldiȝ: ex tantis rei sunt* (*Cura Pastoralis* ed. Sweet 44, l. 22) and *se þe ofslihþ biþ dome scyldiȝ: qui occiderit reus erit iudicio* (Matthew v, 21, MS C.C.C. cxl; *domes*, Hatton MS) But in the four other instances [BT *scyldiȝ* Ia(2) and V(2)] there can be no such contextual explanation. Thus whilst either of these two possibilities may have been the original cause of this uncommon use of the dative, that it resulted in a genuine construction must be recognized.

ȝif þu ȝeþafian nelt   þinȝrædenne,
modȝes ȝemanan.   Micel is þæt onȝin
7 þreaniedlic   þinre ȝelican,
þæt þu forhycȝe   hlaford urne."
130   Him þa seo eadȝe   aȝeaf ondspare,
ȝleap 7 ȝode leof,   Iuliana:
"Ic þe to soðe   secȝan pille,
bi me lifȝendre   nelle ic lyȝe fremman:
næfre ic me ondræde   domas þine,
135   ne me peorce sind   pitebroȝan,
hildepoman,   þe þu hæstlice,
manfremmende,   to me beotast,
ne þu næfre ȝedest   þurh ȝedpolan þinne
þæt þu mec acyrre   from Cristes lofe."
140   Ða pæs ellenpod,   yrre 7 reþe,
frecne 7 ferðȝrim,   fæder pið dehter.
Het hi þa spinȝan,   susle þreaȝan,
pitum pæȝan,   7 þæt pord acpæð:
"Onpend þec in ȝepitte,   7 þa pord oncyr
145   þe þu unsnyttrum   ær ȝespræce,
þa þu ȝoda ussa   ȝield forhoȝdest."
   Him seo unforhte   aȝeaf ondspare
þurh ȝæstȝehyȝd,   Iuliana:
"Næfre þu ȝelærest   þæt ic leasinȝum,
150   dumbum 7 deafum   deofolȝieldum,

(128) *þreaniedlic* Ed, MS *þrea med lic*.

---

(138) *næfre ȝedest*. Holthausen and von der Warth transpose the word order for metrical reasons, whilst Frucht unwarrantably assumes -*dest* to be dissyllabic. Sievers in *Altgermanische Metrik* § 85, n. 4, however, admits three examples in *Beowulf* of alliteration on the second stress of type B, so, even if S. O. Andrew's contention, that such precise formulation of metrical 'rules' is invalid (*Postscript to Beowulf* ch. 10), be not admitted, there are nevertheless no grounds for emendation.

(150) The identification of idols with the devil was patristically orthodox and widely common in OE literature. *Dumbum ond deafum* (*Vita, surdis et mutis*), and to a lesser extent ll. 216 f, is reminiscent of Psalm cxxxv, 15–18. cf the quotation from this psalm in the letter of Pope Boniface, Bede, *Historia Ecclesiastica* II x.

ȝæste ȝeniðlum   ȝaful onhate,
þam pyrrestum   pites þeȝnum,
ac ic peorðiȝe   puldres Ealdor
middanȝeardes   7 mæȝenþrymmes,
155 7 him anum to   eal biþence,
þæt he mundbora   min ȝepeorþe,
helpend 7 hælend   pið hellsceaþum."
    Hy þa þurh yrre   Affricanus,
fæder fæmnan aȝeaf   on feonda ȝepeald,
160 Heliseo.   He in ærinȝe
ȝelædan het   æfter leohtes cyme
to his domsetle: duȝuð pafade
on þære fæmnan plite,   folc eal ȝeador.
Hy þa se æðelinȝ   ærest ȝrette,
165 hire brydȝuma,   bliþum pordum:
"Min se spetesta   sunnan scima,
Iuliana!   Hpæt, þu ȝlæm hafast,
ȝinfæste ȝiefe,   ȝeoȝuðhades blæd!
Ȝif þu ȝodum ussum   ȝen ȝecpemest,
170 7 þe to spa mildum   mundbyrd secest,
hyldo to halȝum,   beoð þe ahylded fram
praþe ȝeporhtra   pita unrim,
ȝrimra ȝyrna,   þe þe ȝeȝearpad sind,
ȝif þu onsecȝan nelt   soþum ȝieldum."
175   Him seo æþele mæȝ   aȝeaf ondspare:
"Næfre þu ȝeþreatast   þinum beotum,
ne pita þæs fela   praðra ȝeȝearpast,

(171) *hyldo* Grein, MS *yldo*.

___

(151) *ȝæste*. Most editors emend, whilst BT assume an exceptional construction of *ȝeniþla* with the dative, and Schaar the influence of the Latin adnominal dative. *Ȝæste* is, however, simply a late spelling. cf Introduction 3. Holthausen (*Anglia*) suggests *ȝæstes*.

(160) *he in ærinȝa*. The omission of the pronominal object is syntactically permissible when the reference is clear. cf l. 227, and for a list of examples in *Beowulf* see Klaeber xcii, n. 9.

(171b–172) 'Innumerable torments, cruelly performed, shall be averted from you'. For this use of the p.pt. of *pyrcan*, cf *me na ne lyst mid glase ȝeworhtra waga* (*De Consolatione Philosophiæ* [Alfred's version] ed. Sedgefield 11, 27).

28

þæt ic þeodscype þinne lufie,
buton þu forlæte þa leasinʒa,
180 peohpeorðinʒa, 7 puldres Ʒod
onʒyte ʒleaplice, ʒæsta Scyppend,
Meotud moncynnes, in þæs meahtum sind
a butan ende ealle ʒesceafta."
    Ða for þam folce, frecne mode,
185 beotpordum spræc, bealʒ hine spiþe
folcaʒende, 7 þa fæmnan het
þurh niðpræce nacode þennan,
7 mid speopum spinʒan synna lease.
Ahloʒ þa se hererinc, hosppordum spræc:
190 "Þis is ealdordom uncres ʒepynnes
on fruman ʒefonʒen! Ʒen ic feores þe
unnan pille, þeah þu ær fela
unpærlicra porda ʒespræce,
onsoce to spiðe þæt þu soð ʒodu
195 lufian polde. Þe þa lean sceolan
piþerhycʒendre, pitebroʒan,
æfter peorþan, butan þu ær piþ hi

(188) *spinʒan*, ʒ altered from a 'c'. (196) *piþerhycʒendre* Ed (except
Thorpe), MS *piþer hycʒen de*.

(190 f) The Acta has *ecce principium quæstionis* with which may be
compared *Seinte Juliene, þis is a biginnunge of þe sar þ tu schalt . . .
drehen* (216 f). As Trautmann first pointed out, Cynewulf probably mis-
took *principium* for *principatus* (hence the rather awkward use of
ealdordom), and interpreted *quæstio* as 'controversy'. Trautmann's
emendation of *on fruman ʒefonʒen* to *on foran ʒeʒonʒ* is, however, based
on a mistaken analogy with the Latin. Translate: 'the supremacy in our
struggle has been seized at the outset'.

(191) *feores*. Von der Warth would insert *nu* after *þe* on the grounds
that in Cynewulf's poems the diphthong in the oblique cases of *feorh* is
always short; cf also l. 508 for which von der Warth suggests [*to*] *pidan
feore*. The only evidence for his contention occurs in the *Elene*, but is
slight in that, as they stand, ll. 680b and 134b are respectively Dx and
A with anacrusis in the second half-line, both uncommon types, but not
without parallel; whilst the phrase *to pidan feore*, which occurs twice,
may owe its quantity to the reduction under a single accent common in
such adverbial phrases. No instance is sufficiently incontrovertible to
justify an emendation in *Juliana*.

29

ȝeþinȝiȝe,   7 him þoncpyrþe
æfter leahtorcpidum   lac onsecȝe,
200 sibbe ȝesette.   Læt þa sace restan,
laÐ leodȝepin.   Ȝif þu lenȝ ofer þis
þurh þin dolpillen   ȝedpolan fylȝest,
þonne ic nyde sceal,   niþa ȝebæded,
on þe þa ȝrimmestan   ȝodscyld precan,
205 torne teoncpide,   þe þu tælnissum
piþ þa selestan   sacan onȝunne,
7 þa mildestan   þara þe men piten,
þe þes leodscype   mid him lonȝe bieode."
Him þæt æþele mod   unforht oncpæÐ:
210 "Ne ondræde ic me   domas þine,
apyrȝed pomsceaÐa,   ne þinra pita bealo;
hæbbe ic me to hyhte   heofonrices Þeard,
mildne Mundboran,   mæȝna Þaldend,
se mec ȝescyldeÐ   piÐ þinum scinlace
215 of ȝromra ȝripe,   þe þu to ȝodum tiohhast.
Ða sind ȝeasne   ȝoda ȝehpylces,
idle, orfeorme,   unbiþyrfe,
ne þær freme meteÐ   fira æniȝ,

(204) þe þa Cosijn, MS þære. (218) meteÐ Ed, MS metet.

---

(203) niþa. Genitive used as instrumental; cf l. 462 and Beowulf 845, 1439 and 2206.

(204) on þe þa ȝrimmestan (MS on þære ȝrimmestan). Von der Warth's interpretation, which refers ȝrimmestan to Juliana (an der grimmigsten [sc. sünderin] die Schuld gegen Gott rächen), is unsatisfactory as there is no recorded instance of ȝrim: sinful, whilst Schaar's suggestion that this phrase is an ellipsis for on þære ȝrimmestan pisan is no better, for the only parallel to such an idiomatic expression which he quotes from Psalm cxl, 8, on pisum provides no satisfactory support for it. Trautmann's emendation is therefore the only reasonable solution. The mistake may possibly have arisen through the transposition of þe þa to þa þe (both of which would be written as one word in the MS), and thence to þare 7 þære.

(208) mid him. Trautmann and von der Warth would omit these words. Undoubtedly, whether read as part of the first or second half-line, they produce a metrical type unrecognized by Sievers, and sound clumsy even to the modern ear. It is, however, too arbitrary to omit them from the text on these grounds.

soðe sibbe, þeah þe sece to him
220 freondrædenne; he ne findeð þær
duʒuþe mid deoflum. Ic to Dryhtne min
mod staþeliʒe, se ofer mæʒna ʒehpylc
paldeð pideferh, puldres Aʒend,
siʒora ʒehpylces: þæt is soð Cyninʒ."
225 Ða þam folctoʒan fracuðlic þuhte,
þæt he ne meahte mod oncyrran,
fæmnan foreþonc. He bi feaxe het
ahon 7 ahebban on heanne beam,
þær seo sunsciene sleʒe þropade,
230 sace sinʒrimme, siex tida dæʒes,
7 he ædre het eft asettan,
laðʒeniðla, 7 ʒelædan bibead
to carcerne. Hyre pæs Cristes lof
in ferðlocan fæste bipunden, ·
235 milde modsefan, mæʒen unbrice.
Ða pæs mid clustre carcernes duru
behliden, homra ʒepeorc; haliʒ þær inne
pærfæst punade. Symle heo Þuldorcyning
herede æt heortan, heofonrices Ʒod,
240 in þam nydcleafan, Nerʒend fira,
heolstre bihelmad; hyre pæs Haliʒ Ʒæst
sinʒal ʒesið.
        Ða cpom semninʒa
in þæt hlinræced hæleða ʒepinna,
yfeles ondpis; hæfde enʒles hip,
245 ʒleap ʒyrnstafa, ʒæstʒeniðla,
helle hæftlinʒ, to þære halʒan spræc:

(240) *nydcleafan*, MS *nyd clafan*.

---

(219) *þeah þe*. See note to l. 42.
(227) *he bi feaxe*. cf note to l. 160.
(244) *enʒles hip*. The *Vita* has *in figura angeli*. This idea, probably of
Rabbinic origin, received orthodox Christian sanction from St Paul,
2 Corinthians xi, 14. It is several times repeated, with didactic intention,
by Gregory I (e.g. *Moralia* xxix, 30), and passed again into Anglo-Saxon
literature in *Genesis B*, from some apocryphal source, such as the *Vita
Adæ et Evæ* or the *Apocalypse of Moses*.

31

"Hpæt dreoȝest þu,   seo dyreste,
7 seo peorþeste   Þuldorcyninȝe,
Dryhtne ussum?   Ðe þes dema hafað
250 þa pyrrestan   pitu ȝeȝearpad,
sar endeleas,   ȝif þu onsecȝan nelt,
ȝleaphycȝende,   7 his ȝodum cpeman.
Þes þu on ofeste,   spa he þec ut heonan
lædan hate,   þæt þu lac hraþe
255 onsecȝe siȝortifre,   ær þec spylt nime,
deað fore duȝuðe;   þy þu þæs deman scealt,
eadhreðiȝ mæȝ,   yrre ȝedyȝan."
    Fræȝn þa fromlice,   seo þe forht ne pæs,
Criste ȝecpeme,   hponan his cyme pære.
260 Hyre se præcmæcȝa   pið þinȝade:
"Ic eom enȝel Ȝodes   ufan siþende,
þeȝn ȝeþunȝen,   7 to þe sended,
haliȝ of heahþu.   Þe sind heardlicu,
pundrum pelȝrim,   pitu ȝeteohhad
265 to ȝrinȝpræce.   Het þe Ȝod beodan,
Bearn Þaldendes,   þæt þe burȝe þa."
    Ða pæs seo fæmme   for þam færspelle
eȝsan ȝeaclad,   þe hyre se aȝlæca,
puldres piþerbreca,   pordum sæȝde.
270 Onȝan þa fæstlice   ferð staþelian,
ȝeonȝ ȝrondorleas,   to Ȝode cleopian:
"Nu ic þec, beorna Hleo,   biddan pille,

(271–2) *to ȝode cleopian | nu ic þec* Grein, MS *to cleopianne ic þec.*

---

(255) *siȝortifre.* The MS form may be regarded as an instrumental, although Cosijn's emendation to the accusative *siȝortifer* may be correct, since such a confusion might easily occur through the similarity of sound.

(265) *ȝrinȝpræce.* There is no need to emend with Holthausen to *ȝrin-*; cp *ȝrunȝon, Elene* 126.

(271) *to Ȝode cleopian: | Nu* (MS *to cleopianne*). Although the correct method of restoring the alliteration to this half-line must remain conjectural, the supplying of *ȝode* and the emendation of *-ne* to *nu*, which most editors agree on, is very plausible, and certainly preferable to Ettmüller's emendation of *cleopianne* to such an inapposite word as *ȝeddjanne.*

32

ece ælmihtiȝ,   þurh þæt æþele ȝesceap
þe þu, Fæder enȝla,   æt fruman settest,
275 þæt þu me ne læte   of lofe hpeorfan
þinre eadȝife,   spa me þes ar bodaðˑ
frecne færspel,   þe me fore stondeðˑ.
Spa ic þe, bilpitne,   biddan pille
þæt þu me ȝecyðˑe,   cyninȝa Þuldor,
280 þrymmes Hyrde,   hpæt þes þeȝn sy,
lyftlacende,   þe mec læreðˑ from þe
on stearcne peȝ."   Hyre stefn oncpæðˑ,
plitiȝ of polcnum,   pord hleoþrade:
"Forfoh þone frætȝan   7 fæste ȝeheald,
285 oþþæt he his siðˑfæt   secȝe mid ryhte,
ealne from orde,   hpæt his æþelu syn."
  Ða pæs þære fæmnan   ferðˑ ȝeblissad,
domeadiȝra.   Heo þæt deofol ȝenom

. . . .

"ealra cyninȝa Cyninȝ   to cpale syllan.
290 Ða ȝen ic ȝecræfte   þæt se cempa onȝon
Þaldend wundian   (peorud to seȝon),
þæt þær blod 7 pæter   bu tu ætȝædre
eorþán sohtun.   Ða ȝen ic Herode
in hyȝe bispeop   þæt he Iohannes bibead

(286) *ealdne, d* subpuncted. (294) *bispeoþ* Gollancz, MS *bispeoþ*.

_____

(280) *sy.* The metre here requires a dissyllabic form; cf Bede's *Death Song* 2, and *Beowulf* 682, 1831, 2649. There is unfortunately no evidence as to the date at which the word became a monophthong, nor as to whether the earlier dissyllabic form was preserved as a poetic archaism.

(288) *domeadiȝra.* A late spelling; cf notes to l. 34, etc.

(288) A folio has here been lost from the MS, cf Introduction 1. In the corresponding passage in the *Vita*, Juliana compels the devil to confess that he is Belial, and that it was he who led Adam to fall, Cain to slay Abel, and many others to commit various crimes (which are enumerated) up to the time when he incited Judas to betray Christ.

(294) *bispeoþ* (MS *bispeoþ*). The emendation to *bispeoþ* is preferable to *bispeon,* since the construction with the latter would be doubtful, whilst that with *bispapan*—and also the figurative use of the word—is paralleled in the *Historia Ecclesiastica* (ed. Miller 128, 26–7): *Ȝif hpylc sy... þæt Rædualde on mod bespape* (*si qui sit, qui Redualdo suadeat...*). For the same palaeographical error cf *Beowulf* 2854 (*speoþ* for *speop*), etc.

33

295 heafde biheapan, ða se halʒa þer
þære piflufan þordum styrde,
unryhtre æ. Eac ic ʒelærde
Simon searoþoncum þæt he sacan onʒon
þiþ þa ʒecorenan Cristes þeʒnas,
300 7 þa halʒan þeras hospe ʒerahte
þurh deopne ʒedþolan, sæʒde hy drys pæron.
Neþde ic nearobreʒdum þær ic Neron bispeac,
þæt he acpellan het Cristes þeʒnas,
Petrus 7 Paulus. Pilatus ær
305 on rode ahenʒ rodera Þaldend,
Meotud meahtiʒne, minum larum.
Spylce ic Eʒias eac ʒelærde

(301) *drys* Sievers, MS *dryas*. (307) *spylce*, *e* inserted above the *c* in
a different hand and ink.

(295–297a) This is an amplification of the *Vita*, which has only: 'ego
sum qui feci ab Herode Joannem decapitari'. It is based directly on Matthew xiv, 4, 'Dicebat enim illi [Herod] Joannes: non licet tibi habere eam'.

(297a–304) The conflict between Peter, assisted by Paul, and Simon
Magus, and their consequent martyrdom under Nero, was a popular
theme of Anglo-Saxon homiletic literature. It is told in the 15th Blick-
ling Homily (EETS lviii, 170–93), Ælfric's homily, 'Passio Apostolorum
Petri et Pauli' (*Homilies* ed. Thorpe 364–84), and Wulfstan's homily,
'de Temporibus Anticristi' (account of Peter and Paul on pp. 98–101 of
Napier's edition). All are based on a Latin original such as the 'Passio
Sanctorum Apostolorum Petri et Pauli', *Acta Petri, Acta Pauli, etc*, ed.
R. A. Lipsius.

(301) *sæʒde hy drys* (MS *dryas*) *pæron*. The *Vita's* equivalent is
'locutus sum quia magi essent'. In the 15th Blickling Homily (p. 173) it
is explained that the followers of Simon Magus turned the apostle's
accusation against their leader back on himself: 'þonne sægdon þa men
þe Simone folgodan þæt Petrus wære dry, þæt ilce þæt Simon him sylf
wæs.' The word *dry* derives from Old Irish *drui*. For an account of its
Celtic ancestry and classical forms and usage see A. Holder, *Alt-celtischen
Sprachsatz*, s.v. *druida*. The MS form here has to be emended, for, as
Sievers has pointed out, the metre requires a monosyllabic form.
Although *drys* (nom.pl.) is not recorded, *drys* (gen.sg.), *dry* (dat.sg.), and
drym (dat.pl.), are found beside the uncontracted forms. It is therefore
likely that the earlier reading here was *drys*, which was later expanded
to the full form. For a long account see Jente § 166.

(307) The name Egias is supplied by Cynewulf, as the *Vita* has only
'ego sum qui Andream feci tradi in regione Patras'. Egias is also men-

JULIANA

þæt he unsnytrum Andreas het
ahon haliȝne on heanne beam,
310 þæt he of ȝalȝan his ȝæst onsende
in puldres plite. Þus ic praðra fela
mid minum broþrum bealpa ȝefremede,
speartra synna, þe ic asecȝan ne mæȝ,
rume areccan, ne ȝerim pitan,
315 heardra heteþonca." Him seo halȝe oncpæð
þurh ȝæstes ȝiefe, Iuliana:
"Þu scealt furþor ȝen, feond moncynnes,
siþfæt secȝan, hpa þec sende to me."
Hyre se aȝlæca aȝeaf ondspare,
320 forht afonȝen, friþes orpena:
"Hpæt, mec min fæder on þas fore to þe,
hellparena cyninȝ, hider onsende
of þam enȝan ham, se is yfla ȝehpæs

(313) asecȝan Ed (except GW), MS asenȝan. (322) -parena, MS perena
with a inserted above the first e in a different hand and ink.

---

tioned in the *Fates of the Apostles* (l. 17). The crucifixion of St Andrew
by order of Egias, a judge in Achaia, is narrated by Ælfric in his homily,
'Natale Sancti Andreæ Apostoli' (*Homilies* ed. Thorpe 576–99), which
derives from one of the various apocryphal Acts of Andrew, such as the
Πράξεις και μαρτυρίον του άγιου άποστόλου 'Ανδρέου printed in the *Acta
Apostolorum* ed. C. Tischendorf. cf Brooks, p. 119.

(313) asecȝan (MS asenȝan). The MS form does not make sense here,
since there is no evidence that senian or its compound could mean anything but to make the sign of the Cross or to bless. The phrase ic asecȝan
ne mæȝ is a common formula, cf l. 494, and *Crist* 221, 1176, etc.

(320) forht afonȝen. No explanation of this half-line is really satisfactory. Strunk's punctuation of it as asyndetic parataxis (afonȝen: cap-
tured) gives sense in this context, but not at *Crist* 1183; the compound
forhtafonȝen accepted by Krapp and others is very dubious; finally,
GK's afon: timor afficere postulates a semantic development for the word
not found elsewhere, but the possibility of its having developed this
meaning is suggested by the analogous collocation forht afæred Phoenix
525 and forhte afærde Crist 893, Andreas 1340; cf forhte 7 afærde, Vercelli
Hom. iv, 214.

(321) hpæt mec min fæder. Holthausen for metrical reasons would
supply Satan after fæder, citing the parallel passage in the Vita: B.
Juliana dixit: Quis te misit ad me? Dæmon respondit: Satanas pater meus.
But type A3 with an exceptional shortening of the second lift is not
unique: see Sievers, *Altgermanische Metrik* § 85, n. 5.

35

in þam ჳrornhofe   ჳeornfulra þonne ic.

325 Þonne he usic sendeð   þæt þe soðfæstra
þurh misჳedpield   mod oncyrren,
ahpyrfen from halor,   þe beoð hyჳeჳeomre,
forhte on ferðþe.   Ne biþ us frea milde,
eჳesful ealdor,   ჳif þe yfles noht

330 ჳedon habbaþ;   ne durran þe siþþan
for his onsyne   oþer ჳeferan.
Þonne he onsendeð   ჳeond sidne ჳrund
þeჳnas of þystrum,   hateð þræce ræran,
ჳif þe ჳemette sin   on moldpeჳe,

335 oþþe feor oþþe neah   fundne peorþen,
þæt hi usic binden   7 in bælpylme
suslum spinჳen.   Ჳif soðfæstra
þurh myrrelsan   mod ne oðcyrreð,
haliჳra hyჳe,   þe þa heardestan

340 7 þa pyrrestan   pitu ჳeþoliað
þurh sarsleჳe.   Nu þu sylfa meaht
on sefan þinum   soð ჳecnapan,
þæt ic þisse noþe þæs   nyde ჳebæded,
þraჳmælum ჳeþread,   þæt ic þe sohte."

345 Þa ჳen seo halჳe onჳon   hæleþa ჳepinnan,
prohtes pyrhtan,   pordum friჳnan,
fyrnsynna fruman: "Þu me furþor scealt

(325) þe Ed, MS se. (334) ჳemette Frucht, MS ჳe mete. (338) ne
oðcyrreð Ed (except Thorpe), MS neod cyrreð. (340) ჳeþoliað, i subpuncted.

---

(338) myrrelsan. This is a nonce word, but nouns with the suffix -els
normally belong to the masc. a-stems. The form therefore may either be
a rare example of a dative denoting cause after þurh (cf BT, þurh, B,
II, i), with confusion of -an and -um (cf Seafarer 48, etc), or more probably the word has gone over to the fem. weak declension. In support of
the latter cf rædels in the De Consolatione Philosophiæ translated by
Alfred (ed. Sedgefield 63, 27) sio rædelse, and rædelsan (100, 25, and
145, 31).

(340) þoliað (with i subpuncted in the MS). Both context and metre
require the plural form; the corrector, who made the error, may perhaps
have come from the area of origin of the Vespasian Psalter Gloss, in
which weak verbs of class II appear without 'i' in the plural.

secȝan, sapla feond,   hu þu soðfæstum
þurh synna slide   spiþast sceþþe,
350 facne bifonȝen."   Hyre se feond oncpæð,
præcca pærleas,   pordum mælde:
"Ic þe, eadmæȝden,   yfla ȝehpylces
or ȝecyðe   oð ende forð,
þara þe ic ȝefremede,   nalæs feam siðum,
355 synna pundum,   þæt þu þy speotolicor
sylf ȝecnape   þæt þis is soð, nales leas.
Ic þæt pende   7 pitod tealde
þriste ȝeþoncȝe,   þæt ic þe meahte
butan earfeþum,   anes cræfte,
360 ahpyrfan from halor,   þæt þu Heofoncyninȝe
piðsoce, siȝora Frean,   7 to sæmran ȝebuȝe,
onsæȝde synna fruman.   Þus ic soðfæstum

(348) *soðfæstum, soðfæst* at the end of one line, *tum* at beginning of next. (350) One or two letters erased after *hyre*. (352) *eadmæȝden*, MS *ead mæȝ*. (354) *siðum* Grein, MS *sindon*.

---

(352) *ic eadmæȝden...or ȝecyðe* (MS *ic ead mæȝ...*). None of the emendations and interpretations proposed hitherto is satisfactory. That of Ettmüller who reads *eaðe...ȝecyðan* involves too extensive an alteration, whilst Gollancz's *eadmæȝ* (cf *pynmæȝ, Guþlac* 1345), and Krapp's acceptance of *ead* as a form of the adjective (cf *Exodus* 186 where *ead* should surely be emended to *ealde*, although Irving keeps the MS reading), provide sense but do not restore the metre. Trautmann's *eadȝe* is preferable, though the scribal error of confusing noun with adjective is unusual. The mistake of writing *mæȝ* for its common synonym *mæȝden* (cf l. 608), however, is more understandable, and so it may be conjectured that the original reading here was *eadmæȝden*, a plausible compound, although it does not occur elsewhere; but cf *gliwmædena*, Ps. 67, 26 (ed. F. Roeder).

(354) *nalæs feam siðum* (MS *sindon*). Thorpe suggested *nalæs fea sindon* as a parenthesis, whilst later editors have preferred to emend *sindon* to *siðum*. The latter is better stylistically (the phrase occurs also in *Elene* 818 and *Andreas* 605), and such a corruption could have arisen through the combination of a number of common palaeographical errors: confusion over 'd' and 'ð', the use of the tilde, and the form of final unaccented syllables.

(358) *ȝeþoncȝe.* This is a reverse spelling. *nȝ* when final was unvoiced at an early date, and written *nc, ncȝ*, etc (Sievers § 215 and n. 1), the *ȝ* being often retained despite the new pronunciation. The spellings thus appeared interchangeable, and hence this type of form found sporadically throughout OE texts.

þurh mislic bleo   mod oncyrre:
þær ic hine finde   ferð staþelian
365 to Jodes willan,   ic beo ȝearo sona
þæt ic him moniȝfealde   modes ȝælsan
onȝean bere   ȝrimra ȝeþonca,
dyrnra ȝedpilda,   þurh ȝedpolena rim.
Ic him ȝespete   synna lustas,
370 mæne modlufan,   þæt he minum hraþe,
leahtrum ȝelenȝe,   larum hyrað.
Ic hine þæs spiþe   synnum onæle
þæt he byrnende   from ȝebede spiceð,
stepeð stronȝlice,   staþolfæst ne mæȝ
375 fore leahtra lufan   lenȝe ȝepunian
in ȝebedstope.   Spa ic broȝan to
laðne ȝelæde   þam þe ic lifes ofonn,
leohtes ȝeleafan;   7 he larum pile
þurh modes myne   minum hyran,
380 synne fremman,   he siþþan sceal
ȝodra gumcysta   ȝeasne hpeorfan;
ȝif ic æniȝne   ellenrofne
ȝemete modiȝne   Metodes cempan
pið flanþræce,   nele feor þonan
385 buȝan from beadupe,   ac he bord onȝean
hefeð hyȝesnottor,   haliȝne scyld,
ȝæstlic ȝuðreaf,   nele Jode spican,
ac he, beald in gebede,   bidsteal ȝifeð

(371) *hyrað*. A late spelling, cf. note to l. 38, etc.

(375) *lenȝe*. cf *Guþlac* 20 and 138 (for both of which emendations have been proposed), and also the gloss *lenge-swiðor-awa* (Wright, *Vocabularies* ed. Wülcker, 495, 13), and the phrase *a hu lenge swiður* (*Vespasian Psalter Gloss*, Psalm cxviii, 107, *Oldest English Texts*, ed. Sweet 367). The number of occurrences make it unnecessary to emend the reading here with Strunk to *lenȝ*.

(378) *ond*. An unusual use of the co-ordinating conjunction in the sense of 'if'. With this usage may be compared MHG *unde* (cf C. Kraus, *Zeitschrift für deutsches Altertum* xliv 149 ff), and possibly ON *enda*, which Vigfusson thought to be identical with *and*, whilst Sievers suggested that it might be a reduced form of *enn þo*. In ME *and* (later *an*) is frequently used for 'if', but the first recorded instance in the NED is from Laȝamon's *Brut* (c. 1205) 8313, *And þu hit nult ileuen...ich hit wulle trousien.*

fæste on feðan,   ic sceal feor þonan,
390 heanmod hþeorfan,   hroþra bidæled,
    in ȝleda ȝripe,   ȝehðu mænan,
    þæt ic ne meahte,   mæȝnes cræfte,
    ȝuðe piðȝonȝan;   ac ic ȝeomor sceal
    secan oþerne,   ellenleasran
395 under cumbolhaȝan,   cempan sænran,
    þe ic onbryrdan mæȝe   beorman mine,
    aȝælan æt ȝuþe.   Þeah he ȝodes hpæt
    onȝinne ȝæstlice,   ic beo ȝearo sona,
    þæt ic inȝehyȝd   eal ȝeondplite,
400 hu ȝefæstnad sy   ferð innanpeard,
    piþersteall ȝeporht;   ic þæs pealles ȝeat
    ontyne þurh teonan;   bið se torr þyrel,
    inȝonȝ ȝeopenad,   þonne ic ærest him
    þurh earȝfare   in onsende
405 in breostsefan   bitre ȝeþoncas,
    þurh mislice   modes pillan,
    þæt him sylfum   selle þynceð
    leahtras to fremman   ofer lof Jodes,
    lices lustas.   Ic beo lareop ȝeorn
410 þæt he monþeapum   minum lifȝe,

(400) ȝefæstnad Ed, MS ȝe fæsnad. (401) piþer- Holthausen, MS pið.

---

(401) piþersteall (MS piðsteall). The MS form is only supported by
the gloss piðsteallas (Wright, Vocabularies ed. Wülcker 461, 23), since
piþfeohtend, a variant of piþerfeohtend, which is found a few times in
prose, as a pres.pt. no doubt owes the unstressed form of the prefix to
its origin from a verb. The emendation piþer- is therefore necessary
(Holthausen's piȝsteall is much less likely). The error may have arisen
through general carelessness or from a confusion over the abbreviation
for r, er, which is not used by the scribes of the Exeter Book, but may
have occurred in their original.

(410) monþeapum. Strunk and some earlier editors have preferred
mánþeapum, a more expressive compound in the context, and similar in
kind to mánpeorc, mándæd, etc. Monþeap, however, occurs at Guþlac 507
and Azarias 190, in both of which the rendering 'evil custom' would be
unsuitable, and this compound survives into ME, cf monþewes, Proverbs
of Alfred, ed. Borgstrom, ll. 431–2. Only at Elene 929 is there another
instance where the rendering 'evil customs' is possible, and in fact preferable. Since the MS word is substantiated by parallels, however, and

39

JULIANA

acyrred cuðlice   from Cristes æ,
mod ʒemyrred,   me to ʒepealde
in synna seað.   Ic þære saple ma,
ʒeornor ʒyme   ymb þæs ʒæstes forpyrd,
415 þonne þæs lichoman,   se þe on leʒre sceal
peorðan in porulde   pyrme to hroþor,
bifolen in foldan."

                    Ða ʒien seo fæmne spræc:
"Saʒa, earmsceapen,   unclæne ʒæst,
hu þu þec ʒeþyde,   þystra stihtend,
420 on clænra ʒemonʒ?   Þu pið Criste ʒeo
pærleas punne   7 ʒepin tuʒe,
hoʒdes wiþ halʒum;   þe pearð helle seað
niþer ʒedolfen,   þær þu nydbysiʒ
fore oferhyʒdum   eard ʒesohtes.
425 Þende ic þæt þu þy pærra   peorþan sceolde
pið soðfæstum   spylces ʒemotes
7 þy unbealdra,   þe þe oft piðstod
þurh Þuldorcyninʒ   pillan þines."
Hyre þa se perʒa   pið þinʒade,
430 earm aʒlæca: "Þu me ærest saʒa
hu þu ʒedyrstiʒ   þurh deop ʒehyʒd
purde þus piʒþrist   ofer eall pifa cyn,
þæt þu mec þus fæste   fetrum ʒebunde,
æʒhpæs orpiʒne.   Þu in ecne Ᵹod,
435 þrymsittendne,   þinne ʒetreopdes,
Meotud moncynnes,   spa ic in minne fæder,
hellparena cyninʒ,   hyht staþelie.

(437) -parena, MS perena with a inserted above the first e in a
different hand and ink.

---

makes sense as it stands, there seems insufficient reason to emend it,
though the possibility remains that an original reading mān- has been
ost through an omitted accent in the MS.
(412) mod ʒemyrred. The phrase may be taken as a parenthesis, and
Holthausen's emendation to mode is not essential, although the resulting
parallel with the preceding line would be pleasing stylistically.
(425) þæt. Trautmann and von der Warth would omit this word. See
note to l. 208.

40

Þonne ic beom onsended   wið soðfæstum,
þæt ic in manþeorcum   mod oncyrre,
440 hyӡe from halor,   me hwilum biþ
forþyrned þurh piþersteall   willan mines,
hyhtes æt halӡum,   swa me her ӡelamp
sorӡ on siþe.   Ic þæt sylf ӡecneow
to late micles;   sceal nu lanӡe ofer þis,
445 scyldwyrcende,   scame þropian.
Forþon ic þec halsiӡe   þurh þæs Hyhstan meaht,
Rodorcyninӡes ӡiefe,   se þe on rode treo
ӡeþrowade,   þrymmes Ealdor,
þæt þu miltsiӡe   me þearfendum,
450 þæt unsæliӡ   eall ne forweorþe,
þeah ic þec ӡedyrstiӡ   7 þus dolwillen
siþe ӡesohte,   þær ic swiþe me
þyslicre ær   þraӡe ne wende."
    Ða seo wlitescyne   wuldres condel
455 to þam wærloӡan   wordum mælde:
"Þu scealt ondettan   yfeldæda ma,
hean helle ӡæst,   ær þu heonan mote,
hwæt þu to teonan   þurhtoӡen hæbbe
micelra manweorca   manna tudre
460 deorcum ӡedwildum."   Hyre þæt deofol oncwæð:
"Nu ic þæt ӡehyre   þurh þinne hleoþorcwide,
þæt ic nyde sceal,   niþa ӡebæded,
mod meldian,   swa þu me beodest,
þreaned þolian;   is þeos þraӡ ful stronӡ,
465 þreat ormæte.   Ic sceal þinӡa ӡehwylc
þolian 7 þafian   on þinne dom,

(453) *wende*, MS *ӡe wende* with *ӡe* subpuncted. (456) *ondettan*, MS *7 dettan*.

---

(457) *helle ӡæst*. These words are usually read as one, although the first element of a compound is normally uninflected. Because of the inevitable lack of evidence, it seems better to treat all such groups as composed of separate words, rather than to guess at possible compounds, when they are not demanded by the sense. Wright in his illustration of these compounds (§ 619) is extremely conservative.

(462) *niþa*. Cf note to l. 203.

JULIANA

pomdæda onþreon,   þe ic þideferȝ
speartra ȝesyrede.   Oft ic syne ofteah,
ablende bealoþoncum   beorna unrim
470 monna cynnes,   misthelme forbræȝd
þurh attres ord   eaȝna leoman
speartum scurum,   7 ic sumra fet
forbræc bealosearpum,   sume in bryne sende,
in liȝes locan,   þæt him lasta pearð
475 siþast ȝesyne;   eac ic sume ȝedyde
þæt him banlocan   blode spiopedan,
þæt hi færinȝa   feorh aleton
þurh ædra pylm.   Sume on yðfare
þurdon on peȝe   pætrum bisencte,

(467) þe Thorpe, MS þy. (468) oft Ed, MS of. (479) on peȝe Frucht, MS onpeȝ.

---

(467) þe (MS þy). The MS reading does not give good sense: the devil will suffer everything at Juliana's discretion because he is niþa ȝebæded (1. 462), not because (þy) he has sinned. The emendation of þy to þe is simpler and more satisfactory stylistically than the insertion of þe before þy. The error may have arisen through a scribe, intent on normalizing the Anglian forms to WSax, mistaking þe (relative particle) for þe the Anglian form of þy (def.art.inst.).

(471) ord. Both Hart and Strunk emend the MS reading to oroð, quoting in support Beowulf 2523, [o]reðes ond attres (by hendiadys 'venemous breath'), Solomon and Saturn 222, attres oroð, and Riddle 60, where ord occurs twice in two lines, one of which must presumably be emended, and might therefore be cited as a parallel instance of the supposed error, although Herzfeld's suggestion of emending one of the occurrences to ecȝ is almost equally plausible. But the phrase in Beowulf is too different in construction to suggest a verbal echo at all strongly, and there is no reason to prefer the statement that the misthelm consisted of poisonous vapour to the statement that the physical cause of the blindness was the poisoned tip of a spear. For the MS phrase cf Maldon 47, ættryne ord, and Crist 768, where attres ord is again used of the shafts of the devil.

(474b–475a) The poet perhaps had a confused recollection of Beowulf 1402 f: BT translate: 'so that no trace of them was left'; literally: 'so that the last of their tracks was seen'.

(479) on peȝe (MS on peȝ). Both sense and metre require the emendation. The scribe perhaps omitted the e by confusion with the adverb onpeȝ, which does not give sense here. Since the metre demands a long vowel, peȝe must be from pæȝ: wave (with non-WSax ē for æ), not from

42

480 on mereflode, minum cræftum,
      under reonʒe stream; sume ic rode bifealh,
      þæt hi heorodreorʒe on hean ʒalʒan
      lif aletan; sume ic larum ʒeteah,
      to ʒeflite fremede, þæt hy færinʒa
485 ealde æfþoncan ednipedan,

(481) *reonʒe*, MS *reone*. (482) *heoru-* GW, MS *hyra*. (485) *ealde* Ettmüller, MS *eald*.

peʒ way. There is no need to emend *on* to *æfter* with Cosijn, since *on peʒe* is parallel to *on yþfare* and *on mereflode*, whilst the word expressing 'in the water' is *pætrum*.

(481) *reonʒe* (MS *reone*). Krapp derives *reone* from *hreoh*, despite the need for alliteration on the *r*. But 'h' disregarded before a consonant would suggest a date for the composition of the poem far later than is borne out by the other evidence. Ettmüller proposed *rynestream* (cf *streamryne*), but no compound with *ryne* as the first element is recorded, and—a more forcible point—it would be difficult to explain the transition of *reone* to *ryne*. It is more probable that *reone* should be derived from *reoniʒ* 'gloomy', cf. l. 530, *in þam reonʒan ham*. The phrase *reonʒe stream* is of the same type as *ʒeomre lyft*, *Exodus* 431.

(482) *heorodreorʒe* (MS *hyra dreorʒe*). Strunk and Krapp retain the MS reading. This assumes, however, either an extraordinarily strained syntax if *hyra* qualifies *lif*, as Krapp supposes, or a very odd turn of phrase if it qualifies *dreorʒe*, and either way a serious weakness in the metre. Grein's emendation to *heoru-* must therefore be accepted, or possibly *heoro-*, since that is the form of the word at ll. 567 and 586, although 'u' and 'a' would be more easily confusable in the MS. The scribal error was probably caused, as Sisam notes (RES xxii 264), by a confusion between *heoru-* and *heora*, which was later replaced by the common WSax form of the pronoun, without back mutation, usual in this poem.

(484) *fremede*. Although *fremman* is occasionally used in the transitive sense 'advance' (BT *fremman* I, *Supplement* II), the meaning required here of 'urge' or 'bring to' would, if accepted, be unique. On the other hand, Schaar's suggestion of 'bring about' (with a comma after *ʒeflite*) involves two rare, though not unparalleled phenomena, those of the simplex form of the verb acquiring the perfective force of its compound with *ʒe*, and of a pause interrupting the unit of the half-line. Of the two possibilities the former is preferred, however, since the sentence rhythm, which requires *to ʒeflite* as a parallel of *larum*, gives it some support.

(485) *ealde æfþoncan* (MS *eald*). Although the two words may constitute a compound not recorded elsewhere, as Gollanz assumes, it seems more likely that the MS form should be emended to *ealde*, since the final *e*, which would not have been pronounced, might easily have been omitted by a scribe copying from dictation; cf *Judith* 265a.

beore druncne;   ic him byrlade
proht of peȝe,   þæt hi in pinsele
þurh speordȝripe   saple forletan,
of flæschoman   fæȝe scyndan,
490 sarum ȝesohte.   Sume þa ic funde
butan Ꝺodes tacne,   ȝymelease,
unȝebletsade,   þa ic bealdlice
þurh mislic cpealm   minum hondum
searoþoncum sloȝ.   Ic asecȝan ne mæȝ,
495 þeah ic ȝesitte   sumerlonȝne dæg,
eal þa earfeþu   þe ic ær 7 siþ
ȝefremede to facne,   siþþan furþum pæs
rodor aræred   7 ryne tunȝla,
folde ȝefæstnad   7 þa forman men,
500 Adam 7 Æve,   þam ic ealdor oðþronȝ,
7 hy ȝelærde   þæt hi lufan Dryhtnes,
ece eadȝiefe,   anforleton,
beorhtne boldpelan,   þæt him bæm ȝepearð
yrmþu to ealdre   7 hyra eaferum spa,
505 mircast manpeorca.   Hpæt sceal ic ma riman
yfel endeleas?   Ic eall ȝebær,
praþe prohtas   ȝeond perþeode,
þa þe ȝepurdun   pidan feore
from fruman porulde   fira cynne,
510 eorlum on eorþan.   Næs æniȝ þara

(486) *druncne* Ed, MS *drucne*. (492) *þa* Thorpe, MS *þeah*. (508) *ȝepurdun* Ettmütter, MS *ȝe pordun*. (510) *næs* Strunk, MS *ne pæs*.

---

(492) *þa* (MS *þeah*). To avoid the strained interpretations proposed by von der Warth and Schaar, *þeah* must be emended to *þa*.

(495) *sumerlonȝne*. cf *winterstunde*, *Gen. B*. 370.

(506) *eall*. The adjective agrees with *yfel* in the previous sentence, and *praþe prohtas* is in apposition: 'Why should I further recount endless evil? I originated it all, the wicked crimes amongst the nations.'

(508) *pidan feore*. See note to l. 191. Krapp observes that this phrase also occurs without the preposition in *Precepts* 23.

(510) *næs* (MS *ne pæs*). The metre requires the emendation, since double anacrusis in type A in the second half-line is extremely doubtful; cf ll. 513a and 518b.

þæt me þus þriste,   spa þu nu þa,
haliჳ, mid hondum   hrinan dorste;
næs æniჳ þæs modiჳ   mon ofer eorþan
þurh halჳe meaht,   heahfædra nan,
515 ne pitჳena;   þeah þe him peoruda Ჳod
onpriჳe, puldres Cyninჳ,   pisdomes ჳæst,
ჳiefe unmæte,   hpæþre ic ჳonჳ to þam
aჳan moste.   Næs æniჳ þara
þæt mec þus bealdlice   bendum bileჳde,
520 þream forþrycte,   ær þu nu þa
þa miclan meaht   mine oferspiðdest,
fæste forfenჳe,   þe me fæder sealde,
feond moncynnes,   þa he mec feran het,
þeoden of þystrum,   þæt ic þe sceolde
525 synne spetan;   þær mec sorჳ bicpom,
hefiჳ hondჳepinn.   Ic bihlyhhan ne þearf
æfter sarpræce   siðfæt þisne
maჳum in ჳemonჳe,   þonne ic mine sceal
aჳiefan, ჳnornceariჳ,   ჳafulrædenne
530 in þam reonჳan ham.''
                    Ða se ჳerefa het,
ჳealჳmod ჳuma,   Iulianan
of þam enჳan hofe   ut ჳelædan,
on hyჳe halჳe,   hæþnum to spræce

---

(511) *þu*, *þ* altered from a 'p'. (519) *bendum* Thorpe, MS *bennum*.
(521) *miclan* Ed, MS *miclam*; *mine* von der Warth, MS *min*.   (533)
haliჳe, i subpuncted.

---

(511) *þæt* (MS *þ̄*). The neuter pronoun is loosely used here for the
masculine. Possibly the original reading here was *þe*, which in an earlier
MS was written as *þ̄*, an abbreviation only used for *þæt* in the *Exeter
Book*, and which should therefore have been expanded; cf also l. 519.

(519) *bendum* (MS *bennum*). cf *Daniel* 434 and *Andreas* 1038. Despite
these three examples, the MS reading can hardly be accepted, with
Krapp, as a genuine variant spelling. The error probably arose through
the *d* being lost in pronunciation by the tenth century; for a discussion
and other examples of this phenomenon see G. C. Langenhove, *On the
Origin of the Gerund in English*, p. 62. But cf Campbell 484.

(521) *mine* (MS *min*). An error arising from the elision of the final *e*.
cf note to l. 485.

to his domsetle. Heo þæt deofol teah,
535 breostum inbryrded, bendum fæstne,
haliᴣ, hæþenne. Onᴣan þa hreopceariᴣ
siðfæt seofian, sar cpanian,
pyrd panian, pordum mælde:
"Ic þec halsiᴣe, hlæfdiᴣe min,
540 Iuliana, fore ᴣodes sibbum,
þæt þu furþur me fraceþu ne pyrce,
edpit for eorlum, þonne þu ær dydest,
þa þu oferspiþdest þone snotrestan
under hlinscuan, helparena cyninᴣ,
545 in feonda byriᴣ; þæt is fæder user,
morþres manfrea. Hpæt, þu mec þreades
þurh sarsleᴣe; ic to soþe pat
þæt ic ær ne sið æniᴣ ne mette
in poruldrice pif þe ᴣelic,

---

(534) *heo, o* altered from a 't'. (544) *-parena* Ed (except Thorpe), MS *perena*. (545) *is* Ed, MS *his*. (549) *pif* Grein, MS *piþ*.

(534 ff) *þæt*. The use of both possible genders of *deofol* in one sentence is unusual, but not without parallel; cf *þ þæs þæt deofol þ seo þeod hyre ær for ᴣod beeodon* 7 *hi nemdon þone astaroð* (King Alfred's *Book of Martyrs* ed. Cockayne *The Shrine* 120, 21–2).

(541 ff) This inexplicable reference to Juliana's defeat of the king of hell occurs in the *Vita* ('Patrem meum superasti, me vinxisti, quid adhuc vis?') and Cynewulf appears to have repeated it uncritically. The difficulty is farther increased in the Anglo-Saxon by the ambiguity of *hlinscua*, which might either refer to Juliana's prison, or to hell, as a variant of *feonda byriᴣ*. It is interesting to notice that in the Munich text of the *Vita* printed by Brunöhler [Münchener cod. Lat. 2570, Brunöhler s (Ml)], this inconsistency is not present, as the corresponding sentence is 'Superasti me, quid aliud vis?' It may be that this apparent inconsistency derives from a version in which Juliana was tempted on two occasions by two distinct fiends; but it is perhaps more likely that the Latin, at least, refers to a vicarious defeat of the prince of devils.

(544) *-parena* (MS *perena*). cf ll. 322 and 437 where a corrector has inserted an 'e' above the *a*, and also *Crist* 731.

(549) *pif (piþ)*. There is no recorded example of *ᴣelice* being construed with *piþ*, and anyway a preposition could not bear the accent and alliteration.

550 þristran geþohtes ne þpeorhtimbran
   mægþa cynnes. Is on me speotul
   þæt þu unscamge æghpæs purde
   on ferþe frod." Ða hine seo fæmne forlet
   æfter þræchpile þystra neosan
555 in speartne grund, sapla gepinnan,
   on pita forpyrd. Þiste he þi gearpor,
   manes melda, magum to secgan,
   susles þegnum, hu him on siðe gelomp.

(555) *gepinnan* Thorpe, MS *gepinna*.

---

(550) *þpeorhtimbran*. Strunk and GK derive this word from *þpeorhtieme*, the latter claiming it to be equivalent to the Latin *ferox* (*Vita* 12). But *þpeorhtieme* occurs only once in OE in the *De Consolatione Philosophiæ* (Alfred's version, ed. Sedgefield 114, 27), where it is used in the sense of 'contentious' or 'quarrelsome', whereas the meaning of *ferox* in its context is 'fierce', the opposite of *misericordes*, and anyway in the OE poem at this point the devil is not reproaching Juliana, as in the Latin sentence cited by GK, but praising her. The compound must therefore be assumed to be a nonce word (thus the difficulty of accounting for an intrusive 'b' is also removed), with the sense 'resolutely made', cf *þpeorlice*, and *magutimber* where *-timber* seems to have the force of an abstract suffix.

(555) *gepinnan* (MS *gepinna*). No satisfactory explanation of the MS form has been provided. It is very unlikely that it is either a Northumbrian form, as Trautmann supposed (on this see Bülbring § 557 and n.), or an instance of the phenomenon found in the Hatton MS of the *Cura Pastoralis*, as Tupper accepted (on this see Sweet's Introduction to his edition of this work, xxxii f). It is simplest to assume a scribal error over the tilde, which in an earlier MS might have been used for 'n' as well as 'm', and which here might have been accidentally omitted by a scribe who would normally have expanded it. For similar omissions see *Juliana* 628 and *Beowulf* 60, etc.

(558-9) A folio has here been lost from the MS; cf note to l. 288, and Introduction 1. The outline of the missing passage according to the *Vita* is as follows: in answer to a question of Eleusius concerning her endurance of torture, Juliana replies that God sent an angel to comfort her, and warns Eleusius of future torments prepared for him. Eleusius thereupon orders her to be placed on a wheel affixed with swords and with flames around it; an angel, however, comes down from heaven and releases her. After Juliana has uttered a prayer of thanksgiving to God, her executioners are converted, and later for this reason beheaded by order of the Emperor Maximian. Eleusius then commands that Juliana be burnt alive, whilst she prays that her enemy may not triumph over her.

. . . .
ȝeorne ær

560 heredon on heahþu 7 his haliȝ weorc,
    sæȝdon soðlice þæt he siȝora ȝehpæs
    ofer ealle ȝesceaft ana peolde,
    ecra eadȝiefa." Ða cpom enȝel Ȝodes
    frætpum blican 7 þæt fyr tosceaf,
565 ȝefreode 7 ȝefreoðade facnes clæne,
    leahtra lease, 7 þone liȝ topearp,
    heoroȝiferne, þær seo halie stod,
    mæȝþa bealdor, on þam midle ȝesund.
    Þæt þam peliȝan pæs peorc to þolianne,

(560) *peorc* supplied by Holthausen. (562) *peolde* Grein, MS *polde*.

(559–63). These lines cannot be the conclusion of the prayer referred to in the last sentence of the preceding note, as Krapp assumes, since God is spoken of in the third person. Von der Warth has argued, on account of the plural verbs, that Cynewulf combined the second torture of burning with the first of the fiery, sword-embedded wheel, and that these lines are part of the prayer of the converted heathen. This view, however, involves the improbable assumption that the beheading of the executioners has been omitted and that they were in fact converted before the miraculous intervention of the angel. Furthermore, the word *ær* suggests that the action of these lines takes place in the past. The most reasonable interpretation is to assume that these words are the conclusion of a speech addressed by Juliana to Heliseus (that Cynewulf should have replaced Juliana's prayer from the flames by a glorification of God's ways spoken to Heliseus is not improbable), and that the verbs refer to holy men from the Bible or church history, whose situations she might be likening to her own, cf her references to Moses, David, etc, in Section 15 of the *Vita*. Holthausen (*Anglia*) proposes *þær* for *ær*.

(560) *peorc*. This word, supplied by Holthausen, is the most plausible of various suggestions, although either *nama* or *dom*, both proposed by von der Warth, or *word* suggested by Cosijn, are quite possible.

(567) *halie*. The form need not be emended with Strunk. of Sievers §214.5.

(569) *þolianne*. Strunk, following Sievers, emends for metrical reasons to *þolian*, whilst S. O. Andrew maintains (§ 157) that all half-lines of this type in *Beowulf*, which appear to be metrically abnormal, should be emended. But the scansion here might be D* (e.g. *Beowulf* 514a, *Altgermanische Metrik* § 84, 7), or A with dissyllabic second thesis (e.g. *Beowulf* 1724b, Sievers in Paul-Braune's *Beiträge* x, 233), and anyway when a rule of uniformity is defined at the cost of emending all exceptions to it, it is at least open to suspicion. The MS reading therefore is here retained.

570 þær he hit for porulde þendan meahte;
sohte synnum fah, hu he sarlicast
þurh þa pyrrestan pitu meahte
feorhcpale findan. Næs se feond to læt,
se hine ʒelærde þæt he læmen fæt
575 bipyrcan het pundorcræfte,
piʒes pomum 7 pudubeamum
holte bihlænan. Ða se hearda bibead
þæt mon þæt lamfæt leades ʒefylde,
7 þa onbærnan het bælfira mæst,
580 ad onælan; se pæs æʒhponan
ymbboren mid brondum; bæð hate þeol.
Het þa ofestlice, yrre ʒebolʒen,
leahtra lease in þæs leades pylm
scufan butan scyldum. Þa toscaden pearð
585 liʒ tolysed; lead pide spronʒ,
hat, heoroʒifre: hæleð wurdon acle,
arasad for þy ræse. Þær on rime forborn
þurh þæs fires fnæst fif 7 hundseofontiʒ
hæðnes herʒes. Ða ʒen sio halʒe stod
590 unʒepemde plite; næs hyre ploh ne hræʒl,
ne feax ne fel fyre ʒemæled,
ne lic ne leoþu. Heo in liʒe stod
æʒhpæs onsund, sæʒde ealles þonc
dryhtna Dryhtne. Þa se dema pearð
595 hreoh 7 hyʒeʒrim, onʒon his hræʒl teran,
spylce he ʒrennade 7 ʒristbitade,
pedde on ʒepitte spa pilde deor,
ʒrymetade ʒealʒmod, 7 his ʒodu tælde,

(577) *bihlænan* Ed (except Thorpe), MS *bi lænan*; *hearda* supplied by Thorpe. (586) *hæleð* Ed, MS *æleð*. (598) *ʒrymetade*, first *e* altered from an 'a'.

---

(570) *þær*. For the use of this word in the sense of 'if', see Klaeber, *Anglia* xxix 271 f, and cf H. Meroney, 'Old English "ðær" if', JEGPh, xli 201 ff.

(577) *hearda*. This word is supplied by all editors to complete the sense, although *hæþen*, suggested by von der Warth, would be almost equally satisfactory.

þæs þe hy ne meahtun   mægne piþstondan
600 pifes pillan.   Þæs seo puldres mæg
anræd 7 unforht,   eafoða gemyndig,
Dryhtnes pillan.   Þa se dema het
aspebban, sorgcearig,   þurh speordbite,
on hyge halge,   heafde bineotan
605 Criste gecorene.   Him se cpealm ne þeah,
siþþan he þone fintan   furþor cuþe.
Ða pearð þære halgan   hyht genipad,
7 þæs mægdnes mod   miclum geblissad,
siþþan heo gehyrde   hæleð eahtian
610 inpitrune,   þæt hyre endestæf
of gepindagum   peorþan sceolde,
lif alysed.   Het þa leahtra ful
clæne 7 gecorene   to cpale lædan,
synna lease.   Ða cpom semninga
615 hean helle gæst,   hearmleoð agol,
earm 7 unlæd,   þone heo ær gebond,
apyrgedne,   7 mid pitum spong;
cleopade þa for corþre,   ceargealdra full:
Gyldað nu mid gyrne   þæt heo goda ussa
620 meaht forhogde,   7 mec spiþast
geminsade,   þæt ic to meldan pearð.
Lætað hy laþra   leana hleotan
þurh pæpnes spor,   precað ealdne nið,
synne gesohte.   Ic þa sorge gemon,
625 hu ic bendum fæst   bisga unrim,
on anre niht,   earfeða dreag,
yfel ormætu. '   Þa seo eadge biseah
ongean gramum,   Iuliana,
gehyrde heo hearm galan   helle deofol.

---

(599) *meahtun* Ed (except Thorpe), MS *meahtum*. (605) *him* Klaeber,
MS *hine*. (620) *forhogde* Ed, MS *for hogd*. (628) *Iuliana* Ed, MS
Iulianan.

---

(605) *him* (MS *hine*). In all recorded instances *þeon* in the sense of
'profit' 'avail', is construed with the dative.

(624) *synne gesohte*. GK *conatam*, but more probably refers to the
torturers.

50

630 Feond moncynnes onȝon þa on fleam sceacan,
    pita neosan, 7 þæt pord acpæð:
    "Þa me forporhtum! Nu is pen micel
    þæt heo mec eft pille earmne ȝehynan
    yflum yrmþum, spa heo mec ær dyde."
635 Ða pæs ȝelæded londmearce neah,
    7 to þære stope, þær hi stearcferþe
    þurh cumbolhete cpellan þohtun.
    Onȝon heo þa læran 7 to lofe trymman
    folc of firenum, 7 him frofre ȝehet,
640 peȝ to puldre, 7 þæt pord acpæð:
    "Ȝemunað piȝena Þyn 7 puldres þrym,
    haliȝra Hyht, heofonenȝla Ȝod!
    He is þæs pyrðe þæt hine perþeode
    7 eal enȝla cynn up on roderum
645 herȝen, heahmæȝen, þær is help ȝelonȝ
    ece to ealdre þam þe aȝan sceal.
    Forþon ic, leof peorud, læran pille,
    æfremmende, þæt ȝe eoper hus
    ȝefæstniȝen, þy læs hit ferblædum

(630) *fleam* Ettmüller, MS *flean*. (637) *h* of *þohtun* altered from 'n'.
(640) *acpæð*, tagged *e* for '*æ*'. (649) *ȝefæstniȝen* Holthausen, MS *ȝefæst niȝe*.

(630) *fleam* (MS *flean*). The emendation is required by the sense. The mistake may have arisen through the similarity in sound of 'm' and 'n' when final in unstressed syllables, or as here after a falling diphthong, or possibly through a confusion over the earlier use of the tilde, cf note to l. 555, and for further examples of this type of error cf ll. 521 and 599.

(631) *pita*. Trautmann's emendation to *wica* cannot be accepted since it is not essential to the context; it is, however, pleasing in view of *Beowulf* 125 and 1125, and the fact that 't' and 'c' may easily be confused in the MS.

(641) *pyn...þrym*. For another example of a leonine rhyme cf *Elene* 1248.

(648) cf *Vita* 20, based ultimately on Matthew vii, 24–7.

(649) *ȝefæstniȝen* (MS *ȝefæstniȝe*). Only Strunk and Krapp retain the MS reading, Strunk as a Northumbrian form, and Krapp, citing Bloomfield (JEGPh xxix 100 ff), as a WSax form. But, as Bloomfield shows that the n-less plural subjunctive was already archaic in Alfred's time, it seems unlikely that this should be a fossilized example of it. For the suggestion of Northumbrian see note to l. 555, and also for a similar error over the use of the tilde.

650 pindas topeorpan;   peal sceal þy trumra
   stronᵹ piþstondan   storma scurum,
   leahtra ᵹehyᵹdum.   Ᵹe mid lufan sibbe,
   leohte ᵹeleafan,   to þam lifᵹendan
   stane, stiðhydᵹe,   staþol fæstniað,
655 soðe treope,   7 sibbe mid eop
   healdað æt heortan,   halᵹe rune
   þurh modes myne.   Þonne eop miltse ᵹiefeð
   Fæder ælmihtiᵹ,   þær ᵹe freme aᵹun
   æt mæᵹna Ᵹode,   mæste þearfe
660 æfter sorᵹstafum,   forþon ᵹe sylfe neton
   utᵹonᵹ heonan,   ende lifes.
   Þærlic me þinceð   þæt ᵹe pæccende
   pið hettendra   hildepoman
   pearde healden,   þy læs eop piþerfeohtend
665 peᵹes forpyrnen   to puldres byriᵹ.
   Biddað Bearn Ᵹodes   þæt me Breᵹo enᵹla,
   Meotud moncynnes,   milde ᵹepeorþe,
   siᵹora Sellend.   Sibb sy mid eopic,
   symle soþ lufu.''   Ða hyre sapl pearð
670 alæded of lice   to þam lanᵹan ᵹefean
   þurh speordsleᵹe.
                  Þe se synscaþa
   to scipe, sceohmod,   sceaþena þreate,
   Heliseus,   ehstream sohte,
   leolc ofer laᵹuflod   lonᵹe hpile
675 on sponrade.   Spylt ealle fornom

(658) *freme* supplied by Trautmann.

---

(654) *stiðhydᵹe*. For the loss of the *ᵹ* see Sievers § 214, 3, and cf *Genesis* 2897 (*stiðhydiᵹ*) and *Elene* 121 (*stiðhidiᵹe*).

(658b) A word is missing from the MS. Strunk and Krapp read *frofre*, which is metrically dubious, cf note to l. 510. Trautmann's suggestion of *freme*, which is stylistically preferable to Holthausen's *friþes* or *ᵹefean* (*Anglia Beiblatt* ix, 356), is therefore accepted here.

(661) *ende lifes*. These words cannot constitute a compound, as Holthausen supposed, since, if this were so, *lifes* would have to be emended to *lif*, the object of *neton* normally being in the accusative.

(670) *lang*. On unusual uses of this word see H. C. Wylde, *Essays and Studies* xi 78 ff.

secʒa hloþe 7 hine sylfne mid,
ær þon hy to lande ʒeliden hæfdon,
þurh þearlic þrea. Þær þrittiʒ pæs
7 feopere eac feores onsohte
680 þurh pæʒes pylm piʒena cynnes,
heane mid hlaford, hroþra bidæled,
hyhta lease, helle sohton.
Ne þorftan þa þeʒnas in þam þystran ham,
seo ʒeneatscolu in þam neolan scræfe,
685 to þam frumʒare feohʒestealde
pitedra penan, þæt hy in pinsele
ofer beorsetle beaʒas þeʒon,
æpplede ʒold. Unʒelice pæs
læded lofsonʒum lic haliʒre
690 micle mæʒne to moldʒræfe,
þæt hy hit ʒebrohton burʒum in innan,
sidfolc micel. Þær siðða̋n pæs
ʒeara ʒonʒum Ʒodes lof hafen
þrymme micle oþ þisne dæʒ
695 mid þeodscipe.

                    Is me þearf micel
þæt seo halʒe me helpe ʒefremme,
þonne me ʒedælað deorast ealra,
sibbe toslitað sinhipan tu,
micle modlufan. Min sceal of lice
700 sapul on siðfæt, nat ic sylfa hpider,

---

(678) *þrittiʒ*, MS **XXX**. (687) *beorsetle* Ed (except Ettmüller), MS *beor sele*. (698) *sinhipan* with *i* inserted between the *h* and *p* above the line.

---

(685) -*ʒestealde*. cf note to l. 38, etc.

(687) *beorsetle* (MS *sele*). The MS word must be emended since *ofer* never possesses the sense of 'in'. Although *beorsetle* is a nonce word, it has a close parallel in *Beowulf* 5 (*meodosetla*).

(692) *sidfolc*. Ettmüller and Grein wished to emend to *sið*. But this use of *sid* qualifying a word for 'people' (widespread people, i.e. multitude) is well substantiated. For the actual compound see Psalm cvi, 2, *sidfolcum*: *regionibus* (ed. Thorpe, p. 305), and cf also *pidfolc*, *Genesis* 1638, and *side*, *Crist* 524, *Beowulf* 2347, etc.

(695b) Beginning of the epilogue.

eardes uncyðþu;   of sceal ic þissum
secan oþerne   ærȝepyrhtum,
ȝonȝan iudædum.   Ᵹeomor hpeorfeð
·ᚻ·ᚪ·7·ᚺ· Cyninȝ biþ reþe,
705 siȝora Syllend,   þonne synnum fah,
·ᛗ·ᛈ·7 ᚻ· acle bidað
hpæt him æfter dædum   deman pille
lifes to leane; ᚾ·ᚱ beofað,
seomað sorȝceariȝ.   Sar eal ȝemon,
710 synna punde   þe ic siþ oþþe ær
ȝeporhte in porulde: þæt ic popiȝ sceal
tearum mænan.   Ðæs an tid to læt
þæt ic yfeldæda   ær ȝescomede,

(701) *þissum*, one letter erased after the *i* in the MS.

---

(701) *uncyðþu*. It is unnecessary to emend the MS form to an adjectival one, either *uncyðȝu* with Hart, or *uncyðiȝ* (a more regular form for
this poem) with Holthausen. Schaar's interpretation of *uncyðþu* as 'un-
known country' (he cites *Guþlac* 852 ff in support) is dubious in that it
involves the rendering of *eard* as 'earth', 'world', instead of its more
usual limited sense of 'native land', etc. Von der Warth's suggestion that
uncyðþu is the instrumental of the indeclinable noun meaning 'ignorance' is preferable, and does not result in an excessively strained syntax,
as Krapp maintains. Translate: 'My soul must depart from my body on
a journey, in ignorance to what land (I myself know not whither).'

(702) *ȝonȝan*. The MS reading should not be emended to *ȝeonȝan* with
Grein, nor regarded with Holthausen and Krapp as a variant of it (*die
Jugendsünden des Jünglings*). The sentence may be translated: 'I must
depart from this place, and seek another with my former actions, journey
accompanied by my early deeds.' Cf Apoc. xiv, 13.

(705) *fah*. All editors emend to *fa*, supposing that *eþu* must be followed
by a plural. But if the rune group is equivalent to the name Cynewulf (cf
Introd. 9 ff), the emendation is unnecessary. There is no consistency
of number in the adjectives and verbs associated with the rune-groups.
Acle and *bidað* are plural, *beofað* and *seomað* singular. The explanation
may be that Cynewulf or the copyist first thought of the runes as a
collective group, and afterwards as separate letters (cf Tupper, p. 254).

(707) *deman*. No emendation is necessary, as the subject may be understood from l. 705; for an identical line see *Crist* 803.

(712) *an*. Strunk, following Grein and Gollancz, assumes that *an* here
is equivalent to *on*. But *an* as an adjective gives reasonable sense: 'that
(particular) time was too late'.

þenden ȝæst ⁊ lic   ȝeador siþedan,
715 onsund on earde.   Þonne arna biþearf,
þæt me seo halȝe   þið þone hyhstan Cyninȝ
ȝeþinȝiȝe;   mec þæs þearf monaþ,
micel modes sorȝ.   Bidde ic monna ȝehþone
ȝumena cynnes,   þe þis ȝied præce,
720 þæt he mec neodful,   bi noman minum
ȝemyne, modiȝ,   ⁊ Meotud bidde
þæt me heofena Helm   helpe ȝefremme,
meahta Þaldend,   on þam miclan dæȝe,
Fæder, frofre Ȝæst,   in þa frecnan tid,
725 dæda Demend,   ⁊ se deora Sunu,
þonne seo Þrynis,   þrymsittende,
in annesse   ælda cynne
þurh þa sciran ȝesceaft   scrifeð bi ȝepyrhtum
meorde monna ȝehþam.   Forȝif us, mæȝna Ȝod,
730 þæt þe þine onsyne,   æþelinȝa Þyn,
milde ȝemeten   on þa mæran tid.   Amen.

(723) *miclan* Ed, MS *miclam*.

---

(719) *præce*. The phrase *ȝied precan* is too common and too apposite here to permit any radical emendation of it, as Ettmüller (*sprece*) and Grein (*ræde*) proposed. Since the preterite in this context is not syntactically possible, *præce* must be assumed to be a variation of *prece*.

(728) *þurh þa sciran ȝesceaft*. The meaning of this half-line is unclear. *Ȝesceaft* has hitherto been interpreted as world, but, if so, *sciran* is an exceedingly inapposite epithet in the context, since Cynewulf's emphasis is on the sinfulness of mankind at the Last Judgement. The preferable interpretation therefore is to take *ȝesceaft* as 'decree', i.e. what God has ordained, and *scir*, 'pure', 'radiant', as the adjective used metaphorically [BT *Supplement*, *scir*, *adj.* I (b)], and to translate: 'in accordance with (by virtue of) His glorious will'.

55

SELECT BIBLIOGRAPHY.

See also: B.J. Muir, *The Exeter Book: A Bibliography*, Exeter, 1992.

I. FACSIMILE

1933 R.W. Chambers, *et al.*, eds, *The Exeter Book of Old English Poetry*, London.

II. EDITIONS

1842 B. Thorpe, *Codex Exoniensis*, London, pp. 242–86.
1850 L. Ettmüller, *Engla and Seaxna Scopas and Boceras*, Quedlinburg, pp. 163–78.
1858 C.W.M. Grein, *Bibliothek der angelsächsischen Poesie*, Goettingen, II, pp. 52–71.
1895 I. Gollancz, *The Exeter Book* Part I, Early English Text Society, civ, pp. 242–84.
1897 C.W.M. Grein and R.P. Wülcker, *Bibliothek der angelsächsischen Poesie*, Leipzig, III, pp. 117–39.
1904 W. Strunk, *Juliana*, Boston.
1936 G.P. Krapp and E.K. Dobbie, *The Exeter Book*, London, pp. lxxxix–cxvii, 113–33.

III. TRANSLATIONS

1842 B. Thorpe (see above).
1859 C.W.M. Grein, *Dichtungen der Angelsachsen*, Kassell, ii, pp. 47–66 (into German).
1895 I. Gollancz (see above).
1905 H.S. Murch, 'Translation of Cynewulf's *Juliana*', *JEGPh* v, 303–19.
1910 C.W. Kennedy, *The Poems of Cynewulf translated into English Prose*, London, pp. 129–52.
1926 R.K. Gordon, *Anglo-Saxon Poetry*, London, pp. 182–96.
1982 S.A.J. Bradley, *Anglo-Saxon Poetry*, London, pp. 301–20.

IV. TEXTUAL AND LITERARY STUDIES AND NOTES

1885 E. Sievers, 'Zur Rhythmik des germanischen Alliterationsverses II', H. Paul and W. Braune, *Beiträge zur Geschichte der deutschen Sprache und Literatur* x, ref. to *Juliana*, 517.
1887 P.H.F. Frucht, *Metrisches und Sprachliches zu Cynewulfs Elene, Juliana und Crist*, Greifswald.
1898 M. Trautmann, *Kynewulf der Bischof und Dichter*, Bonn.
1898 P.J. Cosijn, 'Anglo-Saxonica iv', H. Paul and W. Braune, *Beiträge zur Geschichte der deutschen Sprache und Literatur* xxiii, 123–5.

SELECT BIBLIOGRAPHY

1899 R. Simons, *Cynewulfs Wortschatz*, Bonn.

1902 J.M. Hart, 'Allotria II', *MLN* xvii, 231 f.

1903 C. Abbetmayer, *Old English Poetical Motives derived from the Doctrine of Sin*, New York.

1904 F. Klaeber, 'Emendations in Old English Poems', *Modern Philology* II, ref. to *Juliana*, p. 143.

1905 F. Klaeber, 'Cynewulf's Juliana l. 293 f.', *Anglia Beiblatt* xvi, ref. to *Juliana* p. 227.

1906 Carleton Brown, 'The Autobiographical Element in the Cynewulfian Rune Passages', *Englische Studien* xxxviii, 196–233.

1907 F. Holthausen, Review of Strunk's edition of *Juliana*, *Literaturblatt für germanische und romanische Philologie* xxviii, 10–13.

1907 M. Trautmann, *Berichtigungen, Erklärungen und Vermutungen zu Cynewulfs Werken*, Bonn.

1908 J.J. von der Warth, *Metrisch-Sprachliches und Textkritisches zu Cynewulfs Werken*, Halle.

1908 G. Grau, 'Quellen und Verwandtschaften der älteren germanischen Darstellungen des jüngsten Gerichtes', *Studien zur englische Philologie* xxxi, for *Juliana* see 157–62.

1910 G.A. Smithson, *The Old English Christian Epic*, Berkeley, (*Univ. of California Publications in Mod. Phil.* i 4).

1911 F. Tupper, 'The Philological Legend of Cynewulf', *PMLA* xxvi, 235–79

1912 F. Tupper, 'The Cynewulfian Runes of the Religious Poems' *MLN* xxvii, 131–7.

1918 E.A. Kock, 'Jubilee Jaunts and Jottings', *Lunds Universitets Årsskrift* xiv, 2, notes on *Juliana* pp. 53 f.

1932 K. Sisam, 'Cynewulf and his Poetry', *Proceedings of the British Academy*, xviii, 303–24; reprinted in *Studies in Old English Literature*, Oxford, 1953.

1942 S.K. Das, *Cynewulf and the Cynewulf Canon*, Calcutta.

1943 M.M. Dubois, *Les Éléments Latins dans la Poésie Religieuse de Cynewulf*, Paris.

1949 C. Schaar, *Critical Studies in the Cynewulf Group*, Lund, (*Lund Studies in English* xvii).

1953 R.W.V. Elliott, 'Cynewulf's Runes in *Juliana* and *Fates of the Apostles*', *English Studies* xxxiv, 193–204.

1956 G. Storms, 'The Weakening of O.E. Unstressed *i* to *e* and the date of Cynewulf', *English Studies* xxxviii, 104–10.

1956 F. Holthausen, 'Zu den ae. Gedichten der HS. von Vercelli', *Anglia* lxxiii, 276–8.

1959 R.E. Diamond, 'The Diction of the Signed Poems of Cynewulf', *Philological Quarterly* lvii, 228–41.

1966 R. Woolf, 'Saints' lives', E.G. Stanley, ed. *Continuations and Beginnings*, London, pp. 37–66.

1967 K. Faiss, *Gnade bei Cynewulf und seiner Schule*, Tübingen.

1969 K.A. Bleeth, '*Juliana* 647–52', *Medium Ævum* xxxviii, 119–22.

SELECT BIBLIOGRAPHY

1970 J.F. Doubleday, 'The allegory of the soul as fortress in Old English poetry', *Anglia* lxxxviii, 503–8.

1973 D.G. Calder, 'The art of Cynewulf's *Juliana*', *Modern Language Quarterly* xxxiv, 355–71.

1975 D.W. Frese, 'The art of Cynewulf's runic signatures', L.E. Nicholson and D.W. Frese, eds, *Anglo-Saxon Poetry: Essays in Appreciation*, Notre Dame, pp. 312–34.

1975 J. Wittig, 'Figural narrative in Cynewulf's *Juliana*', *Anglo-Saxon England* iv, 37–55.

1976 R.B. Palmer, 'Characterization in the Old English *Juliana*', *South Atlantic Bulletin* xli (4), 10–21.

1978 L.M. Abraham, 'Cynewulf's *Juliana*: a case at law', *Allegorica* iii, 172–89.

1978 C. Schneider, 'Cynewulf's devaluation of heroic tradition in *Juliana*', *Anglo-Saxon England* vii,. 107–18.

1979 M. Bridges, 'Exordial tradition and poetic individuality in five OE hagiographical poems', *English Studies* lx, 361–79.

1979 S. Morrison, 'OE *cempa* in Cynewulf's *Juliana* and the figure of the *miles Christi*', *English Language Notes* xvii, 81–84.

1979 J.A. Weise, 'Ambiguity in Old English poetry', *Neophilologus* lxii, 588–91.

1980 D.G. Bzdyl, '*Juliana* 559–563a', *Notes & Queries* NS xxvii, 100–01.

1980 C. Marino, 'La *Guiliana* et l'*Elena*; una proposta di analisi', *Annali Istituto Universitario Orientale: Filologia Germanica* xxiii, 101–20.

1980 R.C. St-Jacques, 'The cosmic dimensions of Cynewulf's *Juliana*', *Neophilologus* lxiv, 134–39.

1981 D.G. Calder, *Cynewulf*, Boston.

1983 E.R. Anderson, *Cynewulf: Structure, Style, and Theme of his Poetry*, Rutherford, NJ.

1983 R.J. Schrader, *God's Handiwork: Images of Women in Early Germanic Literature*, Westport, Conn.

1984 J.P. Hermann, 'Language and spirituality in Cynewulf's *Juliana*', *Texas Studies in Literature and Language* xxvi, 263–81.

1984 A.H. Olsen, *Speech, Song, and Poetic Craft: the Artistry of the Cynewulf Canon*, New York.

1985 D.G. Bzdyl, '*Juliana*: Cynewulf's dispeller of delusion', *Neuphilologische Mitteilungen* lxxxvi, 165–75.

1986 M. Nelson, '*The Battle of Maldon* and *Juliana*: the language of confrontation', P.R. Brown *et al.*, eds, *Modes of Interpretation in Old English Literature*, Toronto, pp. 137–50.

1986 K. Swenson, 'Wapentake: a realistic detail in Cynewulf's *Juliana*', *Notes & Queries* NS xxxiii, 3–6.

1986 D.M.E. Gillam, 'Love triangle at comedia: some sidelights on Cynewulf's handling of personal relationships in *Juliana*', A.M. Simon-Vandenbergen, ed., *Studies in Honour of René Derolez*, Ghent, pp. 190–215.

SELECT BIBLIOGRAPHY

1990 A.H. Olsen, 'Cynewulf's autonomous women: a reconsideration of Elene and Juliana', H. Damico and A.H. Olsen, eds, *New Readings on Women in Old English Literature*, Bloomington, Ind., pp. 222–32.
1991 M. Nelson, *Judith, Juliana, and Elene: Three Fighting Saints*, New York.
1992 J.D. Wine, 'Juliana and the figures of rhetoric', *Papers on Language and Literature* xxviii, 3–18.

V. THE LEGEND

(*a*) VERSIONS

(These are arranged in chronological order, but, through default of any certainty of the centuries of their composition, the dates given here are of their publication in print.)

1658 'Acta auctore anonymo', *Acta Sanctorum*, ed. Iohannes Bollandus, Godefridus Herschenius, *Februarius Tom.* II 873 ff.
1658 Petrus Subdiaconus, 'Alia Vita', *Acta Sanctorum, Februarius Tom.* II 878 ff.
1658 'Translatio III S. Julianæ', *Acta Sanctorum, Februarius Tom.* II 883 ff.
1861 Simeon Metaphrastes, Μαρτύριον τῆς ʿαγίας μαρτύρος ᾿Ιουλιανῆς τῆς ᾿εν Νικομηδίᾳ, Migne, *Patrologiæ Cursus Completus, Series Græca* cxiv, colls 1437 ff.
1906 *The Legend of St. Juliana translated from the Latin of the Acta Sanctorum and the Anglo-Saxon of Cynewulf*, transl. C.W. Kennedy, Princeton, NJ.
1936 *Þe Liflade ant te Passiun of Seinte Iuliene*, ed. S.T.R.O. d'Ardenne, Liège; reprinted in 1961 as EETS. ccxlviii.
1976 'The Acts [of Juliana]', transl. M.J.B. Allen and D.G. Calder, *Sources and Analogues of Old English Poetry*, Cambridge, pp. 22–32.

Details of other versions will be found in Strunk, pp. xli ff. and p. 65, and in d'Ardenne, p. xvii.

(*b*) CRITICAL DISCUSSIONS

1889 O. Glöde, 'Cynewulfs Juliana und ihre Quelle', *Anglia Zeitschrift für englische Philologie* xi, 146–58.
1899 O. Backhaus, *Über die Quelle der mittelenglischen Legende von der heiligen Juliene, und ihr Verhältnis zu Cynewulfs Juliana*, Halle.
1899 J.M. Garnett, 'The Latin and Anglo-Saxon Juliana', *PMLA* xiv, 279–98.
1912 E. Brunöhler, *Über einige lateinische, englische, französische, und deutsche Fassungen der Julianen-Legende*, Bonn.
1964 T. Wolpers, *Die englische Heiligenlegende des Mittelalters*, Tübingen.
1986 J.G. Price, 'The *Liflade of Seinte Iuliene* and hagiographic convention', *Medievalia et Humanistica* NS xiv, 37–58.

GLOSSARY

In the glossary words will be found under the forms in which they occur in the text, except that nouns and adjectives (excluding irregular comparatives, etc) will be found under the m.nom.sg. or nom.pl., and verbs under the infinitive; pronouns will be under the m.nom.sg. (except that the 1st and 2nd pers. of the personal pronouns will be found under the nom.sg. and nom.pl.). Irregular grammatical or phonological forms likely to offer difficulty are noted in their proper places with cross-references to the words under which they are dealt with. An 'n' after a line reference indicates that the word is discussed in the appropriate note, an 'ᴧ' that it is dealt with in the appendix, and an * that it is a restored or emended form.

The order of the letters is alphabetical: æ is treated as a separate letter after a; þ and ð after t; the prefix ᵹe- is ignored in the arrangement, and verbs with this prefix are only entered separately from the simplex form, when the meaning is distinct.

Reference is made to the *New English Dictionary* by printing the NED word (under which the OE word is discussed) as the first meaning in capitals; if the word is descended from a foreign cognate, a related variant, or from a dialect form different from that recorded in the glossary, it is italicized. Unless it provides the meaning required by the context, it is followed by a semicolon and the required meaning in lower case type. If it is radically different in meaning, or if it is obsolete or archaic, it is enclosed in square brackets. Unless otherwise stated, the NED reference is to the same part of speech as the word in the glossary.

A

ā, *adv.* [O]; ever 183.

āblendan, *w.v.(1b),* [ABLEND]; blind 469.

ac, *conj.* [AC]; but 85, 153, etc.

āclian, *w.v.(2),* terrify (*p.pt.*) 268.

ācol, *adj.* terrified 586, 706.

ācwellan, *w.v.(1c),* [AQUELL]; kill 303.

ācweðan, *v.(5),* [ᴧ + QUETHE]; speak 45, 143, etc.

ācyrran, *w.v.(1b),* [ᴧ + CHARE]; turn away 139, (*p.pt.*) 411.

ād, *m.a-stem,* [AD]; funeral pyre 580.

āfōn, *v.(7),* [AFONG]; seize (*p.pt.*) 320n.

āgalan, *v.(6),* [ᴧ + GALE]; sing 615.

āgan, *pret.-pres.* (7), [OWE]; have, possess 44n, 518, etc.

āgælan, *w.v.(1b),* [ᴧ + GELE]; hinder 397.

āgend, *m.nd-stem,* Lord 223.

āgiefan, *v.(5),* [AGIVE]; give 105, etc, render 529.

āglǽca, *m.n-stem,* [EGLECHE *adj.*]; monster, evil creature 268, etc.

āhebban, *v.(6),* [AHEAVE]; raise 228; wage 4.

āhlyhhan, *v.(6),* [ᴧ + LAUGH]; laugh 189.

āhōn, *v.(7),* [AHANG]; hang 228, etc.

āhwyrfan, *w.v.(1b),* [ᴧ + WHARVE]; turn away 327, 360.

āhyldan, *w.v.(1b),* [ᴧ + HIELD]; avert (*p.pt.*) 171.

ālǣdan, w.v.(1b), [A + LEAD]; lead away (p.pt.) 670.

ālǣtan, v.(7), [ALET]; lose, give up 477, 483.

ālȳsan, w.v.(1b), [ALESE]; set free (p.pt.) 612.

ān, num. ONE 626; adj. alone 104, etc, that 712n; pron. ONE 359; on an, outright 69, adv. prefix 104.

ānforlǣtan, v.(7), forsake 502.

ānga, adj. ONLY 95.

ānnes, f.jō-stem, [ANNES(SE)]; unity 727.

ānrǣd, adj. [ANRED]; resolute 90, 601.

ār, f.ō-stem, [ORE]; favour 81; mercy 715.

ār, m.a.-stem, orig. u.-stem, messenger 276.

ārāsian, w.v.(2), overtake, seize (p.pt.) 587.

ārǣran, w.v.(1b), [AREAR]; raise up (p.pt.) 498.

āreccan, w.v.(1c), [ARECCHE]; relate 314.

ārlēas, adj. [ORE + LESS]; cruel 4.

āsecgan, w.v.(3), [A + SAY]; relate 313*, 494.

āsettan, w.v.(1a), orig. (1c), [ASET]; take down 231.

āstīgan, v.(1), [ASTY(E)]; arise 62.

āswebban, w.v.(1a), [ASWEVE]; put to death 603.

attor, n.a.-stem, [ATTER]; poison 471.

āþum, m.a.-stem, [ODAM]; son-in-law 65.

āwyrg(i)an, w.v.(1b), [AWARIE]; accursed (p.pt.) 211, 617.

Æ

ǣ, f.i-stem, [Æ]; law 13, 411; marriage 297n.

ǣd(e)r, f.ō-stem, vein 478.

ǣdre, adv. forthwith 231.

ǣfre, adv. EVER 81.

ǣfremmende, pres.pt. [Æ + FREME]; fulfilling the law 648.

ǣfter, adv. AFTER, afterwards 197. prep.w.dat. AFTER 78, etc, among, through 11.

ǣfþonca, m.n-stem, grudge 485.

ǣghwā, pron. ǣghwǣs, semi-adv. completely, in every respect 434, etc.

ǣghwonan, adv. on all sides 580.

ǣht, f.i-stem, [AUGHT]; possessions 37.

ǣhtgesteald, n.a-stem, wealth, possessions 115.

ǣhtspēdig, adj. [AUGHT + SPEEDY]; wealthy 101.

ǣhtwelig, adj. [AUGHT + WEALY]; rich 18.

ǣlde, m.i-stem pl. man 727.

ǣlmihtig, adj. ALMIGHTY 273, 658.

ǣnig, adj., pron. ANY 116n*, 218, etc.

ǣpplede, adj. [APPLED]; round (?) 688a.

ǣr, adv. ERE, formerly, before 75, 120, etc, in phrases w. siþ, always 496, 548, 710; ǣrest, superl. first 164, etc; conj. before, 255, 457, 520; prep.w.dat. ǣr þon, before 677.

ǣrgewyrht, f. or n.i-stem, [ERE + IWURHT]; former deed 702.

ǣring, f.ō-stem, daybreak 160.

ǣt, prep.w.dat. AT 274; in 239, etc; from 81, etc.

ǣtgǣdre, adv. together 292.

ǣþele, adj. [ATHEL]; noble 18, etc.

ǣþeling, m.a-stem, [ATHELING]; noble 37, etc.

ǣþelu, n.ja-stem, pl. [ATHEL]; origins 286.

B

bānloca, *m.n-stem*, [BONE + LOKE]; body 476.

bǣdan, *w.v.(1b)*; constrain (*p.pt.*) 203, etc.

bǣlfīr, *n.a-stem*, [BALEFIRE]; funeral fire 579.

bǣlwylm, *m.i-stem*, [BALE + WALM]; surging fire 336.

bærnan, *w.v.(1b)*, BURN 16*.

bæð, *n.a-stem*, BATH; liquid 581.

beadu, *f.wō-stem*, fight 385.

bēag, *m.a-stem*, [BEE]; ring 687.

beald, *adj.* BOLD 388.

bealdlīce, *adv.* BOLDLY 492, 519.

bealdor, *m.a-stem*, chief 568.

bealo, *n.wa-stem*, BALE; evil 211, 312.

bealosearo, *n.wa-stem*, wicked snare 473.

bealoþonc, *m.a-stem*, [BALE + THANK]; evil thought 469.

bēam, *m.a-stem*, BEAM; cross 228, 309.

bearn, *n.a-stem*, [BAIRN]; son 266, 666.

gebed, *n.a-stem*, [I + BEAD]; prayer 373, 388.

gebedstōw, *f.wō-stem*, [I + BEAD + STOW]; place of prayer 376.

bēgen, *adj.* [BO]; both 64; bū tū (*acc.n.*) 292; bǣm (*dat.m.*) 503.

behlīdan, *v.(1)*, [BE + LID]; close (*p.pt.*) 237.

belgan, *v.(3)*, [BELL]; to enrage oneself (*refl.*) 185; *p.pt.* enraged 58, etc.

bend, *m.i-* or *f.jo-stem*, [BEND], BOND 519n*, etc.

bēodan, *v.(2)*, BID, command 265, 463.

beofian, *w.v.(2)*, [BIVE]; tremble 708.

bēon, *anom.v.* BE; eom, 261, bēo, 49, etc, bēom, 438, *1pers.pres.*

sg. eart, 93, *2pers.pres.sg.*; is, 100, etc, biþ, 328, etc., *3pers, pres.sg.*; bēoð, 327, *1pers.pres. pl.*; sind, 71, etc, bēoð, 171; *3pers.pres.pl.*; sȳ, 88, 280n, etc., *pres.subj.sg.*; sȳn, 286, sīn, 334, *pres.subj.pl.*; wes, 253, *imp.sg.*. wæs, 343, *1pers.pret.sg.*; wæs, 8, etc, *3pers.pret.sg.*; wǣron, 64, 301, *3pers.pret.pl.*; wǣre, 259, *pret.subj.sg.* næs, 510n, etc, *neg.3pers.pret.sg.*

bēor, *n.a-stem*, BEER 486.

beorgan, *v.(3)* *w.dat. and acc.* [BERGH]; guard 266.

beorht, *adj.* BRIGHT, glorious 503.

beorma, *m.n-stem*, [BARM]; leaven 396.

beorn, *m.a-stem*, [BERNE]; man 272, (warrior?) 469; nobleman 41.

bēorsetl, *n.a-stem*, [BEER + SETTLE]; bench in the hall 687n*.

bēot, *n.a.-stem*, [BEOT]; threat 176.

bēotian, *w.v.(2)*, [BEOTE(N)]; threaten 137.

bēotword, *n.a-stem*, threat, 185.

beran, *v.(4)*, BEAR 28, 367.

geberan, *v.(4)*, [IBERE]; bring forth, originate, 506.

betra, *comp.adj.* BETTER 100.

bī, *prep.w.dat.* BY 227, 720; according to 728; *w.pt.phrase*, while 133 (see libban).

bibēodan, *v.(2)*, [BE + BID]; command (*p.pt.*) 11, 232, etc.

bīdan, *v.(1)*, BIDE, await 706.

bidǣlan, *w.v.(1b)*, *w.gen.* [BE-DEAL]; *p.pt.* deprived of 390, 681.

biddan, *v.(5)*, BID; pray 272, etc; beseech 718.

bīdsteal, *m.a-stem*, [BIDE + STALL]; a stand 388.

biféolan, v.(3), commit 417, 481.
bifōn, v.(7), [BEFANG]; encompass (p.pt.) 350.
bigān, anom.v. [BEGO]; worship 208.
bigong, m.a-stem, [BE + GANG]; circuit, expanse 112.
bigongan, v.(7), [BE + GANG]; worship 110, 121.
bihēawan, v.(7), [BEHEW]; heafde beheapan, behead 295.
bihelmian, w.v.(2), [BE + HELM]; cover (p.pt.) 241.
bihlǣnan, w.v.(1b), [LEAN]; set around 577*.
bihlyhhan, v.(6), [BE + LAUGH]; laugh, rejoice 526.
bilecgan, w.v.(1c), BELAY, lay upon, cover 519.
bilwit, adj. [BILEWHIT]; gentle 278.
(ge)bindan, v.(3), BIND 336, 433, 616.
binēotan, v.(2), w.acc. and dat. [BE + NAIT]; deprive of 604.
bisencan, w.v.(1b), [BESENCH]; submerge (p.pt.) 479.
bisēon, v.(5), [BESEE]; look 627.
bisgo, f.ō. or n-stem, [BUSY]; affliction 625.
biswāpan, v.(7), [BESWAPE]; incite 294n*.
biswīcan, v.(1), here w. pret. of v.(2), [BESWIKE]; seduce 302.
biter, adj. BITTER; wicked 405.
biþencan, w.v.(1c), BETHINK, confide, entrust 52, 155.
biþurfan, pret.-pres.(3), w.gen. [BE + THARF]; have need 715.
biweddian, w.v.(2), [BEWED]; betroth (p.pt.) 33.
biwindan, v.(3), [BEWIND]; enclose (p.pt.) 234.
biwyrcan, w.v.(1c), [BEWORK]; make 575.
blǣd, m.i-stem, [BLEAD]; glory 168.

blēo, n.ja-stem, [BLEE]; form 363.
blīcan, v.(1), [BLIK(E)]; shine 564.
blissian, w.v.(2), [BLISS]; gladden p.pt. 287, 608.
blīþe, adj. BLITHE, pleasant 165.
blōd, n.a-stem, BLOOD, 7, etc.
bōccræftig, adj. [BOOK+CRAFTY]; learned 16.
bodian, w.v.(2), BODE, announce 276.
bold, n.a-stem, [BOLD]; dwelling, house 41, 114.
boldwela, m.n-stem, [BOLD + WEAL]; happy dwelling-place 503
bord, n.a-stem, BOARD; shield 385.
brād, adj. BROAD, spacious 8.
brecan, v.(4), BREAK; torment 27.
brego, m.u-stem, prince, king 666.
brēost, n.a-stem, (pl. in sq. sense), BREAST 535.
brēostsefa, m.n-stem, mind 405.
brēotan, v.(2), [BRET]; destroy 16n.
(ge)bringan, w.v.(1c), BRING, lead 114, 691.
brōga, m.n-stem, terror, 376.
brond, m.a-stem, BRAND, flame 581.
brōþor, m.r-stem, BROTHER 312.
brȳd, f.i-stem, BRIDE 41.
brȳdguma, m.n-stem, BRIDE-GROOM, suitor 100, 165.
brȳdlufu, f.ō-stem, later n-stem, [BRIDE + LOVE]; conjugal love 114.
bryne, m.i-stem, [BRUNE]; fire, furnace 473.
(ge)būgan, v.(2), BOW; turn, flee, 385; submit, 361.
burg, f.monos.-stem, BOROUGH, town, city 11, etc.
būtan, prep.w.dat. [BOUT]; without 183, etc; conj.w.subj. unless, save that (būton) 179, 197.
bū tū, see bēgen.

byrlian, *w.v.(2),* [BIRLE]; offer (of drink) 486.

byrnan, *v.(3),* BURN 373.

C

carcern, *n.a.-stem,* [CARCER(AL) + EARN]; prison 233, 236.

ceargealdor, *n.a-stem,* [CARE + GALDER]; sorrowful dirge 618A.

ceaster, *f.ō-stem,* [CHESTER]; city 21.

cempa, *m.n-stem,* [KEMP]; warrior 17, etc; soldier 290.

cennan, *w.v.(1b),* [KEN]; *pæs him noma cenned,* his name was 24.

circe, *f.n-stem,* CHURCH 5.

clǣne, *adj.* CLEAN, pure, innocent 31, 420, etc.

cleopian, *w.v.(2),* [CLEPE]; call, cry 271, 618.

clūstor, *n.a-stem,* [CLAUSTER]; bolt 236.

gecnāwan, *v.(7),* [I + KNOW]; KNOW 342, etc.

condel, *f.jō-stem,* CANDLE, light 454.

gecoren, *adj. (p.pt.),* CHOSEN 16, etc.

corþer, *n.a-stem,* multitude 618.

cræft, *m.i-stem,* CRAFT, skill, power, 359, etc.

gecræftan, *w.v.(1b),* [I + CRAFT]; contrive 290.

Crīsten, *adj.* [CHRISTEN]; Christian 5

cuman, *v.(4),* COME 242, etc.

cumbolhaga, *m.n-stem,* [-HAW, cf. HEDGE]; war hedge 395.

cumbolhete, *m.i-stem (orig. -os, -es-stem),* [-HATE]; hateful violence 637

cunnan, *pret.-pres.(3),* [CON], CAN; know 33, etc.

cūðlice, *adv.* [COUTHLY]; certainly, manifestly 411.

cwalu, *f.ō-stem,* [QUALE]; violent death, slaughter 289, 613.

cwānian, *w.v.(2),* bewail 537.

cwealm, *m. or n.a-stem,* [QUALM]; slaying 493, 605.

cwellan, *w.v.(1c),* QUELL; slay 5, 637.

cwelman, *w.v.(1b),* [QUELM]; slay 15.

(ge)cwēman, *w.v.(1b) w.dat.* [QUEME]; please, propitiate 169, 252.

gecwēme, *adj.w.dat* [I + QUEME]; pleasing, acceptable 259.

cweðan, *v.(5),* [QUETHE]; speak 92.

cyme, *m.i-stem,* [COME]; coming 161, 259.

cyn, cynn 644, *n.ja-stem,* KIN; race, tribe 432, etc; lineage 18.

cyning, *m.a-stem,* KING 224, etc; emperor 4.

gecȳðan, *w.v.(1b),* [I + KITHE]; make known, reveal 279, 353.

D

gedafen, *adj.(p.pt.),* suitable 87.

daraðhæbbende, *pres.pt.* holding a spear 68.

dǣd, *f.i-stem,* DEED, action 13, 52, etc.

dǣdhwæt, *adj.* [DEED + WHAT]; bold in deeds 2.

dæg, *m.a-stem,* DAY 2, 230, etc.

gedǣlan, *w.v.(1b),* [I + DEAL]; divide, part 697.

dēaf, *adj.* DEAF 150.

dēað, *m.a.-stem, orig. u-stem,* DEATH 87, etc.

delfan, *v.(3),* DELVE, dig *(p.pt.)* 423.

dēma, *m.n-stem,* [DEME]; judge 249, etc.

dēman, *w.v.(1b),* DEEM; adjudge 707, condemn 87; proclaim 2.

dēmend, *n.nd-stem*, [DEMEND]; judge 725.

dēofol, *m. or n.a-stem*, DEVIL 221, etc.

dēofolgield, *n.a-stem*, [DEVIL + YIELD]; idolatry 52; idol 150.

dēop, *adj.* DEEP, profound 301, 431.

dēor, *n.a-stem*, DEER; wild beast 125, 597.

deorc, *adj.* DARK 460.

dohtor, *f.r-stem*, DAUGHTER 68, etc.

dolwillen *adj.* [DULL + WILLv.]; foolish, rash, 451.

dolwillen, *n.ja-stem*, [DULL + WILLv.]; foolishness, rashness, 202.

dōm, *m.a-stem*, DOOM; judgement, opinion 98; decree 134, 210; will, discretion 466.

dōmēadig, *adj.* [DOOM + EADI]; blessed with glory, 288n.

dōmsetl, *n.a-stem*, [DOOM + SETTLE]; judgement-seat 162, 534.

dōn, *anom.v.* DO 110, etc.

gedōn, *anom.v.* [IDO]; accomplish 138, 330; bring harm 475.

drēogan, *v.(2)*, [DREE]; suffer 247, 626.

drincan, *v.(3)*, DRINK; *p.pt.*, drunk 486*.

drȳ, *m.i.-stem*, DRUID (*though NED does not mention OE form*); sorcerer 301n*.

dryhten, *m.a-stem*, [DRIGHTIN]; Lord 13, etc; lord 594.

duguð, *f.ō-stem*, [DOUTH]; multitude 162, 256; profit, help 221.

dumb, *adj.* DUMB, mute 150.

*durran, *pret-pret.(3)*, DARE 330, 512.

duru, *f.u-stem*, DOOR 236.

gedwild, *n.i-stem*, [I + DWILD]; error 368, 460.

gedwola, *m.n-stem*, [I + DWALE]; error, delusion 202, etc; evil conduct 138.

gedwolen, *adj.* (*p.pt. of *dwelan, cf dwellan*), [DWELL]; perverse 13.

gedȳgan, *w.v.(1b)*, escape 257.

dȳre, *adj.* DEAR, beloved 725, *sup.* 93, etc.

dyrne, *adj.* [DERN]; evil, dark 368.

gedyrstig, *adj.* rash 451; bold 431.

E

ēac, *adv.* EKE; also, likewise 297, 307, etc.

ēadgifu, *f.ō-stem*, [EAD(I) + GIVE]; (gift of) grace 276, etc.

ēadhrēðig, *adj.* blessed 257.

ēadig, *adj.* [EADI]; (*as noun*) blessed (one) 105, etc.

ēadlufu, *f.ō-stem*, later *n-stem*, [EAD(I) + LOVE]; love 104.

ēadmægden, *n.ja-stem*, [EAD(I) + MAIDEN]; blessed maiden 352n*.

eafera, *m.n-stem*, offspring 504.

eafoð, *n.a-stem*, strength (*pl. in sg. sense*) 601.

ēage, *n.n-stem*, EYE 95, 471.

eahtian, *w.v.(2)*, deliberate 609; declare 1.

ēahtnys, *f.jō-stem*, persecution 4n.

eald, *adj.* [ELD]; OLD 485n*, 623.

ealdor, *n.a-stem*, life 124n, 500, etc; *to ealdre*, for ever 504, 646.

ealdor, *m.a-stem*, [ALDER]; prince, lord 153, etc.

ealdordōm, *m.a-stem*, [ALDER-DOM]; dominion, supremacy 25, 190n.

eall, eal, *adj.* ALL 10, 36, etc.

eard, *m.a-stem, orig. u-stem*, [ERD]; land, region 701; earth 715; dwelling 20, 424.

earfeð, *n.a-stem*, earfeðe, *n.ja-stem*, (ARVETH); difficulty, hardship, suffering 359, etc.

eargfaru, *f.ō-stem*, [ARROW + FARE]; flight of arrows 404.

earm, *adj.* [ARM]; wretched 430, etc.

earmsceapen, *adj.* [ARM + SHAPEN]; wretched 418.

ēce, *adj.* [ECHE]; eternal 273, etc; undying 104.

ēce, *adv. ece to ealdre*, for ever and ever 646.

edniwian, *w.v.(2)*, [ED + NEW]; renew 485.

edwīt, *n.a-stem*, [EDWIT]; disgrace 542.

eft, *adv.* [EFT]; again 231, 633.

egesful, *adj.* [EISFUL]; terrible 329.

egsa, *m.n-stew*, [EIS(FUL)]; fear, terror 35, 268.

ēhstrēam, *m.a-stem*, [I(SLAND) + STREAM]; sea 673.

ellenlēas, *adj.* [ELNE + LESS]; *comp.* less courageous 394.

ellenrōf, *adj.* [ELNE-]; brave 382.

ellenwōd, *adj.* [ELNE + WOOD]; furious 140.

elles, *adv.* ELSE, otherwise 113.

ende, *m.ja-stem*, END 183, etc.

endelēas, *adj.* ENDLESS 251, 506.

endestæf, *m.a-stem*, [END + STAFF]; departure 610.

enge, *adj.* narrow 323, 532.

engel, *m.a-stem*, ANGEL, 244, etc.

eodor, *m.a-stem*, [EDDER]; sky 113.

eorl, *m.a-stem*, EARL; (noble, brave) man 510, 542.

eorþe, *f.n-stem*, EARTH, world 44, etc.

ēower, *poss.pron.* YOUR 648.

F

fācen, *n.a-stem*, [FAKEN]; evil 350, etc.

fāh, *adj.* [FOE]; guilty 59, etc.

faran, *v.(6)*, FARE, go 11.

fæder, *m.r-stem*, FATHER 32, etc.

fæge, *adj.* [FEY]; doomed to die 489.

fæmne, *f.n-stem*, maiden 27, etc.

færinga, *adv.* [FEAR-]; with sudden calamity 477, 484.

færspel, *n.a-stem*, [FEAR + SPELL]; sudden (w. connotation of terrible) message 267, 277.

fæst, *adj.* FAST, firmly bound 535, 625.

fæste, *adv.* FAST, firmly 42, etc.

fæstlīce, *adv.* [FAST + LY]; firmly 270.

(ge)fæstnian, *w.v.(2)*, FASTEN; make firm 649*, 654; secure, fortify (*p.p.t.*) 400; establish (*p.pt.*) 499.

fæt, *n.a-stem*, [FAT], VAT; vessel 574.

fēa, *adj.* FEW 354.

feax, *n.a-stem*, [FAX]; hair 227, 591.

fel, *n.a-stem*, FELL, skin 591.

fela, *n.indec.* (orig.u-stem) *w.gen.* [FELE]; many 177, etc.

fēogan, *w.v.(3)*, later (2), persecute 14.

feohgesteald, *n.a-stem*, [FEE-]; riches 685n.

feohgestrēon, *n.a-stem*, [FEE + ISTREON]; treasure 42, 102.

fēond, *m.nd-stem*, FIEND; enemy 159, etc; devil 350, etc.

fēondlīce, *adv.* [FIENDLY]; in hostile manner 118.

fēondscype, *m.i-stem*, [FIENDSHIP]; enmity 14.

feor, *adv.* FAR 335, etc.

feorh, *n.* or *m.a-stem*, orig.u-stem, life 119, etc; *pidan feore*, for ever 508n.

feorhcwalu, *f.ō-stem*, [-QUALE]; violent death 573.

fēowere, *num.* FOUR 679.

(ge)fēran, *w.v.(1b)*, [FERE]; go 523; come 331.

66

GLOSSARY

fērblǣd, *m.i-stem*, [FEAR + BLEAD]; sudden blast 649.

fērend, *m.nd-stem*, messenger 60.

ferð, *m. or n.a-stem*, spirit, mind 270, 287, etc.

ferðgrim, *adj.* [-GRIM]; fierce in mind 141.

ferðloca, *m.n-stem*, [-LOKE]; locked place of the mind 79n, 234.

feter, *f.ō-stem*, FETTER 433.

gefetigan, *w.v.(2)*, [I+FET]; FETCH 60.

fēða, *m.n-stem*, army, company 389.

fīf, *num.* FIVE 588.

findan, *v.(3)*, FIND 81, etc.

finta, *m.n-stem*, sequel 606.

fīras, *m.ja-stem(pl.)*, men 218 etc.

firen, *f.ō-stem*, [FERN?]; sin 639

firencræft, *m.i-stem*, [FERN? + CRAFT]; wickedness 14.

firendǣd, *f.i-stem*, [FERN? + DEED]; crime 59.

flǣschoma, *m.n-stem*, [FLESH + HAME]; body 489.

flānþracu, *f.ō-stem*, [FLANE-]; storm of arrows 384.

flēam, *m.a-stem*, [FLEME]; flight 630*.

geflit, *n.a-stem*, [FLITE]; strife 484.

fnǣst, *m.a-stem*, [FNAST]; blast 588.

folc, *n.a-stem*, FOLK; people 74, etc.

folcāgende, *pres.pt. used as noun*, [FOLK + OWING]; leader 186.

folctoga, *m.n-stem*, leader of the people 225.

folde, *f.n-stem*, [FOLD]; earth 417, 499.

fōn, *v.(7)*, [FANG]; seize, take (*p.pt.*) 98, 191.

fōr, *f.ō-stem*, [FORE]; journey 321.

for, *prep.w.dat.* FOR, before, in front of 184, etc; on account of 267, 587; on, in (*in phrases w. eorþan or porulde*) 95, etc.

forbyrnan, *v.(3)*, [FORBURN]; destroy by fire 587.

forbrecan, *v.(4)*, [FORBREAK]; crush 473.

forbregdan, *v.(3)*, [FORBRAID]; snatch away 470.

fore, *prep.w.dat.* [FORE]; because of, for 31, etc; before, in the presence of 74, etc.

foreþonc, *m.a-stem*, [FORE + THANK]; intention 227.

forfōn, *v.(7)*, [FOR + FANG]; seize 284, 522.

forgifan, *v.(5)*, FORGIVE; grant 729.

forht, *adj.* [cf FRIGHT *n.*]; fearful, afraid 258, etc.

forhycgan, *w.v.(3)*, despise, disdain 129, etc.

forlǣtan, *v.(7)*, [FORLET]; reject 104, 122; abandon 179; give up 488; allow 553.

forma, *adj.* [FORME]; first 499.

forniman, *v.(4)*, [FORNIM]; destroy 675.

forsēon, *v.(5)*, [FORSEE]; despise 44.

forð, *adv.* FORTH, forward 353; still, 121.

forþon, *conj.* [FORTHON]; therefore, consequently 103, etc; because 660.

forþryccan, *w.v.(1c)*, [FOR + THRUTCH]; overwhelm, torment 520

forweorþan, *v.(3)*, [FORWORTH]; perish 450.

forwyrcan, *w.v.(1c)*, [FORWORK]; *p.pt.* ruined, undone 632.

forwyrd, *n.a-stem, orig. f.i.-stem*, [FOR + WEIRD]; destruction 414, 556.

forwyrnan, *w.v.(1b)*, *w.gen. and dat.* FORWARN; deny, hinder 441, 665.

fōt, *m.monos-stem*, FOOT 472.

67

fracoð, *n.a-stem*, [FRAKED *adj.*]; insult 71, 541.

fracuðlic, *adj.* ignominious 225.

frætig, *adj.* wicked, stubborn 284.

frætwe, *f.wō-stem(pl.)*, [FRET?]; adornments 118, 564.

frēa, *m.n-stem*, lord 328; Lord 361.

frēcne, *adj.* fierce, horrible 67, etc; dangerous, terrible 724.

fremde, *adj.* [FREMD]; strange 74, 121.

fremman, *w.v.(1a)*, [FREME]; commit 380, 408; urge 484n; *lyge fremman*, tell a lie 133.

gefremman, *w.v.(1a)*, [1 + FREME]; bring about 119, etc; commit 312, etc; *helpe gefremme*, give help 696.

fremu, *f.in-stem*, *later indec.*, [FREME]; help 123, 218, 658*.

gefrēogan, *w.v.(2)*, orig. (3), [YFREE]; FREE 565.

frēond, *m.nd-stem*, FRIEND 102.

frēondrǣden, *f.jō-stem*, friendship, affection 34, 71n, etc.

gefreoðian, *w.v.* (2), [1 + FRITH?]; protect 565.

frignan, *v.(3)*, [FRAYNE]; ask 258, 346.

frīg, *f.ō-stem*, [cf FRI(DAY)]; love 103.

friþ, *n.a-stem*, orig. *m.u-stem*, [FRITH]; peace 320.

frōd, *adj.* wise 553.

frōfor, *f.ō-stem*, [FROVER]; help 639; comfort 724.

from, *adv.* [FROM]; *from hogde*, despise 34.

from, fram 171, *prep.w.dat.* FROM 139, etc.

fromlīce, *adv.* boldly 89, 258; speedily (*sup.*) 40.

fruma, *m.n-stem*, [FRUME]; beginning 191, etc; author, originator 347, 362.

frumgār, *m.a-stem*, [FRUME + GARE]; leader 685.

ful, *adv.* FULly, very 33, 464.

full, ful, *adj.w.gen.* FULL 612, 618.

furþor, furþur 541, *comp.adv.* FURTHER 317, etc.

furþum, *adv.* [FORTHEN]; first 497.

fylgan, *w.v.(1b)* orig. (3), *w.dat.* *or acc.* FOLLOW 202.

fyllan, *w.v.(1b)*, FELL, destroy 5.

gefyllan, *w.v.(1b)*, *w.gen. of indir. obj.*, FILL with 578+

fȳr, *n.a-stem*, FIRE 564, etc.

fyrnsyn, *f.jō-stem*, [FERN? + SIN]; wicked (or former) crime 347A.

fyrwet, *n.ja-stem*, desire 27.

G

gaful, *n.a-stem*, [GAVEL]; tribute 151.

gafulrǣden, *f.jō-stem*, account 529.

galan, *v.(6)*, [GALE]; sing 629.

galga, *m.n-stem*, GALLOWS, cross 310, 482.

gān, *anom.v.*, GO; ēode (*pret.3sg.*) 89.

gār, *m.a-stem*, [GARE]; spear 17, 63.

gǣlsa, *m.n-stem*, extravagance, lust 366.

gǣst, *m.a-stem*, orig. *-os,-es-stem*, GHOST; spirit, soul 28, 35, etc.

gǣstan, *w.v.(1b)*, persecute 17.

gǣstgehȳgd, *n.a-stem*, orig. *f.i-stem*, thought 148.

gǣstgenīðla, *m.n-stem*, enemy of the soul 245.

gǣstlic, *adj.* GHOSTLY; spiritual 387.

gǣstlīce, *adv.* GHOSTLY; in spirit 398.

gē, *pron.* YE; you 648, etc; ēowic (*acc.*) 668; ēow (*dat.*) 655, 657, 664.

geador, *adv.* TOGETHER 163 (*w. eal.*) 714.

gealgmōd, *adj.* [-MOOD]; cruel 531, 598.

gēar, *n.a-stem,* YEAR 693.

gearo, *adj.* [YARE]; ready, prepared (*w.gen.*) 49, etc.

gearwe, *adv.* [YARE]; readily (*comp.*) 556.

gegearwian, *w.v.(2),* [1 + YARE]; prepare 55, etc.

gēasne, *adj.* [GEASON]; lacking 216; deprived of 381.

geat, *n.a-stem,* GATE 401.

gēaþ, *f.ō-stem,* foolishness 96.

gehōu, *f.ō-stem,* misery 391.

gēn, gīen 417; *adv.* yet 110, etc; moreover 290, 293; again 345

gēo, *adv.* of old 420.

geoguōhād, *m.a-stem, orig. u-stem,* [YOUTHHOOD]; youth 168

gēomor, *adj.* [YOMER]; sad, mournful 393, 703.

geond, *prep.w.acc.* [YOND]; throughout 3, etc.

geondwlītan, *v.(1),* see through 399.

geong, *adj.* (*used as noun*), YOUNG (woman) 35, etc.

georn, *adj.* [YERN]; eager, zealous 39, 409.

georne, *adv.* [YERNE]; earnestly, diligently 29, 559; (*comp.*) 110, 414.

geornful, *adj.w.gen.* [YERN+FUL]; eager, desirous (*comp.*) 324.

gēotan, *v.(2),* [YET]; shed 6.

gied, *n.ja-stem,* [YED]; poem 719.

giefan, *v.(5),* GIVE 85; *bidsteal gifeð,* make a stand 388; show, have (*miltse*), 657.

giefu, *f.ō-stem,* [GIVE]; gift, grace 168, etc.

gield, *n.a-stem,* YIELD; service, worship 146; deity 174.

gegierwan, *w.v.(1b),* prepare 40.

gif, *conj.* IF 47, etc.

ginfæst, *adj.* [-FAST]; ample, abundant, 168.

glædmōd, *adj.* [GLAD + MOOD]; of gentle mind 91n*.

glæm, *m.i-stem,* GLEAM; radiant beauty 167.

glēaw, *adj.* [GLEW, GLEG]; wise 131; having great knowledge (*w.gen.*) 245.

glēawhycgende, *adj.* wise in mind 252.

glēawlīce, *adv.* [GLEW + LY]; clearly 181.

glēd, *f.i-stem,* [GLEED]; burning coal, fire 391.

gnorncearig, *adj.* [-CHARY]; sorrowful 529.

god, *m.a-stem,* GOD 17, 23, etc; *m.* or *n.a-stem,* GOD (heathen) 51, 74, etc.

gōd, *n.a-stem,* GOOD, virtue 216, 397.

gōd, *adj.* GOOD 102, 381.

godhergend, *m.nd-stem,* [GOD + HERY *v.*]; worshipper of God, 6*.

godscyld, *f.i-stem,* [GOD + SHILD(Y) *adj.*]; blasphemy 204.

gold, *n.a-stem,* GOLD 688.

goldspēdig, *adj.* [GOLD + SPEEDY]; wealthy 39.

gong, *m.a-stem,* [GANG]; way, access 517; course (of time) 693.

gongan, *v.(7),* [GANG]; journey 703.

græswong, *m.a.- orig. u-stem,* [GRASS + WONG]; grassy plain 6.

grennian, *w.v.(2),* GRIN; bare the teeth 596.

grētan *w.v.(1b),* GREET, welcome 164.

grim, *adj.* GRIM, fierce, horrible 173, 367, (*sup.*) 204.

gringwracu, *f.ō-stem,* [-WRACK]; deadly punishment 265n.

69

gripe, *m.i-stem*; GRIP, grasp 125, 391; power 215.

gristbitian, *w.v.(2)*, [GRISTBITE]; gnash the teeth, 596.

grom, *adj.* [GRAME]; fierce (as noun) 215, 628.

grondorlēas, *adj.* innocent 271.

grornhof, *n.a-stem*, house of sorrow 324.

grund, *m.a- orig. u-stem*, GROUND; earth 10, 332; abyss 555

grymettan, *w.v.(2)*, rage 598.

guma, *m.n-stem* [GOME]; man 39, etc.

gumcyst, *f.i-stem*, noble virtue 381.

gūð, *f.δ-stem*, battle 393, 397.

gūðreaf, *n.a-stem*, [-REAF]; armour 387.

gyldan, *v.(3)*, YIELD; requite 619.

gȳman, *w.v.(1b)*, *w.gen.* [YEME]; care for 70, 414.

gȳmelēas, *adj.* [YEMELESS]; heedless 491.

gyrn, *f. or n.i-stem*, evil, trouble 173, 619.

gyrnstæf, *m.a-stem*, [-STAFF]; affliction 245.

H

habban, *w.v.(3)*, HAVE (auxil.) 11, etc; have, possess 25, etc; **nabban** (neg.) 77, 116.

hālig, *adj.* HOLY, (or as noun) holy one, saint 7, 15, etc.

hālor, *n.-os, -es-stem*, (dat. of hæl, Sievers § 289, n. 3), 327, etc.

hālsian, *w.v.(2)*, [HALSE]; entreat 446, 539.

hām, *m.a-stem*, HOME, dwelling 323, etc.

hāt, *adj.* HOT, burning 586.

(ge)hātan, *v.(7)*, [HIGHT]; vow, promise 53n, 639; command 60, 74, etc.

hāte, *adv.* HOT, fiercely 581.

hæftling, *m.a-stem*, captive 246.

hælend, *m.nd-stem*, [HEALEND]; saviour 157.

hæleð, *m.eþ-stem*, [HELETH]; man, hero, 243, etc.

hæste, *adj.* violent 56.

hæstlice, *adv.* violently 136.

hæþen, *adj.* HEATHEN (st. used as noun) 7, 64, etc.

hæþenfeoh, *n.a-stem*, [HEATHEN + FEE]; heathen sacrifice 53n*.

hæþengield, *n.a-stem*, [HEATHEN + YIELD]; idol 15, 22.

hē, *pron.m.* HE 11, 22, etc; **hine**, *acc.* 27, 185, etc; **his**, *gen.* 8, 26, etc; **him**, *dat.* 24, 40, etc; **hīo**, **hēo**, *f.* she 28, 34, etc; **hī**, **hȳ**, *acc.* 77, 85, etc; **hire**, **hyre**, *gen.* 30, 32, 165, etc; **hire**, **hyre**, *dat.* 35, 117, etc; **hit**, *n.acc.* IT 570, etc; **hī**, **hȳ**, *nom.pl.* they 12, 63, etc; **hī**, **hȳ**, *acc.* 197, 501; **hyra**, *gen.* 504; **him**, *dat.* 81, 198, etc.

hēafod, *n.a-stem*, HEAD 295, 604.

hēah, *adj.* HIGH, lofty 228, etc; (sup.) **hȳhstan** 446, 716.

hēahfæder, *m.r-stem*, [HIGH + FATHER]; patriarch 514.

hēahmægen, *n.a-stem*, [HIGH + MAIN]; supreme power 645.

hēahþu, *f. often indec.* HEIGHT; of heahþu, from above 263; on heahþu, on high 560.

(ge)healdan, *v.(7)*, HOLD 284; keep, 22, 31, etc.

hēan, *adj.* [HEAN]; wretched 457, etc.

hēanmōd, *adj.* [HEAN + MOOD]; humiliated 390.

heard, *adj.* HARD, severe 56, 315; (sup.) 339; stern (as noun) 577n*.

heardlic, *adj.* [HARD + LY]; severe 263.

hearm, *m.a-stem,* HARM; misery 629.

hearmlĕoð, *n.a-stem,* [HARM + LEOTH]; song of misery 615.

hebban, *v.*(6), HEAVE; raise 386; raise up 15; extol (*p.pt.*) 693.

hefig, *adj.* HEAVY, grievous 526.

hell, *f.jō-stem,* HELL 246, etc.

hellsceaþa, *m.n-stem,* [HELL + SCATHE]; hellish foe 157.

hellwaran, *m.n-stem.pl.* inhabitants of hell 322, etc.

helm, *m.a-stem,* HELM; protector 722.

help, *f.ō-stem,* HELP 645, etc.

helpend, *m.nd-stem,* [HELPEND]; helper 157.

heofon, *m.a-stem,* HEAVEN 112, 722.

heofoncyning, *m.a-stem,* [HEAVEN + KING]; king of heaven 360.

heofonengel, *m.a-stem,* [HEAVEN + ANGEL]; angel of heaven 642.

heofonrīce, *n.ja-stem,* [HEAVEN-RIC]; kingdom of heaven 212, 239.

heolstor, *m.a-stem,* darkness 241.

heonan, *adv.* [HEN]; hence 253, etc.

heorodrēorig, *adj.* [-DREARY]; covered with blood, 482n*.

heorogīfre, *adj.* [-YEVER]; fiercely ravenous 567, 586.

heorte, *f.n-stem,* HEART 239, 656.

hĕr, *adv.* HERE 116, 442.

here, *m.ja-stem,* [HERE]; army 589.

hererinc, *m.a-stem,* [HERE + RINK]; warrior, man 189.

herian, *w.v.*(1a), [HERY]; praise 77, etc.

heteþonc, *m.a-stem,* [HATE + THANK]; thought of hate 315.

hettend, *m.nd-stem,* enemy 663.

hider, *adv.* HITHER 322.

hildeþremma, *m.n-stem,* [-THRUM]; warrior 64.

hildewōma, *m.n-stem,* terror (?) 136, 663. See App. s.v. **woma.**

hildfruma, *m.n-stem* [-FRUME]; leader 7.

hīw, *n.ja-stem,* HUE; form 244.

hlāford, *m.a-stem,* LORD 129, 681.

hlǣfdige, *f.n-stem,* LADY 539.

hlǣnan, *w.v.*(1b), LEAN, incline 63.

hlĕo, *n.wa-stem,* LEE; protector 49, 272.

hlĕotan, *v.*(2), (*w.gen.*) obtain 622.

hlĕoþorcwide, *m.i-stem,* [-QUIDE]; speech 461.

hlĕoþrian, *w.v.*(2), speak 283.

hlīnrӕced, *n.a-stem,* prison 243.

hlīnscūa, *m.n-stem,* [-SCU(?)]; darkness of prison 544n.

hlōþ, *f.ō-stem,* band 676.

hof, *n.a-stem,* dwelling 532.

holm, *m.a-stem,* [HOLM]; ocean 112.

holt, *m.* or *n.a-stem,* HOLT; wood 577.

homor, *m.a-stem,* HAMMER 237.

hond, *f.u-stem,* HAND 493, 512.

hondgewinn, *n.a-stem,* [HAND + IWIN]; struggle 526.

hordgestrēon, *n.a-stem,* [HOARD + ISTREEN]; treasure 22.

hordloca, *m.n-stem,* [HOARD + LOKE]; coffer 43.

hosp, *m.a-stem,* contumely 300.

hospword, *n.a-stem,* contemptuous WORD 189.

hraþe, *adv.* RATHE; quickly 254, 370.

hrӕgl, *n.a-stem,* [RAIL]; robe 590, 595.

hrēowcearig, *adj.* [RUE + CHARY]; sorrowful 536.

hrīnan, *v.*(1), *w.dat.,* [RINE]; touch 512.

hrōþor, *n.-os,-es-stem (dat. of hreþ,* Sievers § 289, n. 1), comfort, joy 390, etc.

hū, *adv.* HOW 34, etc.

hundseofontig, *num.* [HUND + SEVENTY]; seventy 588.

hūs, *n.a-stem*, HOUSE 648.

hwā, hwæt, *inter. pron.* WHO, WHAT 280, 318, etc; *indef. pron.* somewhat 397.

gehwā, *pron.w.part.gen.* WHO; every 323, etc.

hwæt, *interj.* WHAT; lo, behold 1, 167, etc.

hwæþre, *adv.* WHETHER; nevertheless 517.

hweorfan, *v.(3)*, WHARVE; turn away from, depart 275, 381, etc.

hwider, *adv.* WHITHER 700.

hwīl, *f.ō-stem*, WHILE; time 674; *hpilum* [WHILOM]; at times 440.

gehwylc, *pron.w.part.gen.* [IWH-ILLC]; EACH, every 30, etc.

hwonan, *inter.adv.* [WHENNE]; whence 259.

hycgan, *w.v.(3)*, determine 29; plot 422; *from hogde*, despised 34.

gehygd, *f. or n.i-stem*, purpose 431, 652.

hyge, *m.i-stem orig. -os, -es-stem*, [HIGH]; mind, heart 77, etc.

hygeblind, *adj.* spiritually BLIND 61.

hygegēomor, *adj.* [HIGH + YOMER]; sad in mind 327.

hygegrim, *adj.* [HIGH + GRIM]; fierce of mind 595.

hygesnottor, *adj.* [HIGH + SNOTER]; wise in mind 386.

hȳhstan, *see* hēah.

hyht, *m.i-stem*, [HIGHT]; hope, joy 212, 437, etc.

hyldo, hyldu 82, *f.in-stem, later indec.* favour 171.

gehȳnan, *w.v.(1b)*, [I + HEAN; humiliate 633.

hȳran, *w.v.(1b)*, *w.dat.* HEAR 1; obey, follow (*w.dat.*) 371n, 379.

gehȳran, *w.v.(1b)*, [YHERE]; learn by hearing 59, 461, etc.

hyrde, *m.ja-stem*, HERD; guardian 66, 280.

hyrst, *f.i-stem*, jewel 43.

I

ic, *pron.* I 46 etc; mec, mē, *acc.* 53, 74, etc; mē, *dat.* 68, etc.

īdel, *adj.* IDLE, vain 217.

ides, *f.ō-stem*, woman 116.

in, *adv.* IN 404; *prep.w.dat. or acc.* in, into, at 2, 21, etc.

inbryrdan, *w.v.(1b)*, inspire (*p.pt.*) 535.

ingehygd, *f. or n.i-stem*, inward thought, 399.

ingong, *m.a-stem*, [INGANG]; entrance 403.

innan, *adv.* [INNE]; within 691.

innanweard, *adj.* INWARD 400.

inne, *adv.* [INNE]; within 237.

inwitrūn, *f.ō-stem*, [-ROUN]; evil counsel 610.

īudǣd, *f.i-stem*, former DEED 703.

L

lāc, *n.a-stem, or f.ō-stem*, [LAKE]; sacrifice 111, etc.

lācan, *v.(7)*, [LAKE]; bound 674.

laguflōd, *m.a-stem*, flōd, *orig. u-stem*, [-FLOOD]; ocean 674.

lāmfæt, *n.a-stem*, [LOAM + FAT, VAT]; earthen vessel 578.

lār, *f.ō-stem*, LORE; teaching, instruction 306, etc.

lārēow, *m.wa-stem*, [LAREW]; teacher 409.

lāst, *m.a-stem*, LAST; trace 474n.

late, *adv.* LATE 444.

lāþ, *adj.* LOATH; hateful, harmful 201, etc.

lāþgenīðla, *m.n-stem*, foe 232.

(ge)lǣdan, *w.v.(1b)*, LEAD, bring 161, 254, etc.

lǣmen, *adj.* LOAM(ED); earthen 574

(ge)lǣran, *w.v.(1b)*, [LERE]; teach 149, 281, etc.

lǣs, *comp. adv.* LESS; *þy lǣs*, LEST 649, 664.

lǣt, *adj.* LATE 712; slow 573.

lǣtan, *v.(7)*, LET, allow 88, etc.

lēad, *n.a-stem*, LEAD 578, etc.

gelēafa, *m.n-stem*. [YLEVE]; belief, faith 378, 653.

leahtor, *m.a-stem*, [LAHTER]; sin, vice 371, etc.

leahtorcwide, *m.i-stem*, [-QUIDE]; blasphemy 199.

lēan, *n.a-stem*, [LEAN]; retribution, requital 195, etc.

lēas, *adj.* [LEASE]; *(w.gen.)* free from, without 188, etc; false 356.

lēasing, *f.ō-stem*, [LEASING]; a thing which deceives 149, 179.

leger, *n.a-stem*, LAIR; grave 415.

leng, *see* **longe**.

gelenge, *adj.w.dat.* attached to 371

lēodgewinn, *n.a-stem*, [LEDE + IWIN]; strife 201.

lēodscype, *m.i-stem*, [LEDE + SHIP]; people 208.

lēof, *adj.* LIEF; dear, beloved *(sup.)* 84, *(comp.)* 122, etc; pleasing *(comp.)* 88.

lēoht, *n.a-stem*, LIGHT 95, etc.

lēoht, *adj.* LIGHT, clear, shining 378, 653.

lēoma, *m.n-stem*, LEAM; light 471.

leoþu, *see* **liþ**.

libban, *w.v.(3)*, LIVE 410, *(pres.pt.)* 653; *ʒif min feorh leofað*, if I live 119; *bi me lifʒendre*, while I live 133.

līc, *n.a-stem*, [LICH]; body 409, etc.

gelīc, *adj.* [YLIKE]; *þe ʒelic*, thy equal 549.

gelīce, *f.n-stem*, LIKE, equal 128.

līchoma, *m.n-stem*, [LICHAM]; body 415.

līf, *n.a-stem*, LIFE 88, etc.

līg, *m.i-stem*, [LEYE]; fire, flame 17, etc.

gelimpan, *v.(3)*, [ILIMP]; happen 2, etc.

liþ, *n.a-stem*, *orig.* *m.u-stem*, [LITH]; limb 592.

līðan, *v.(1)*, [LITHE]; go, journey *(pt.p.)* 677.

loca, *m.n-stem*, LOKE; embrace 474.

lof, *m. or n.a-stem*, [LOF]; praise, glory 48, 139, etc.

lofian, *w.v.(2)*, [LOVE]; praise 76.

lofsong, *m.a-stem*, [LOFSONG]; song of praise 689.

lond, *n.a-stem*, LAND 677.

londmearc, *f.ō-stem*, LANDMARK; boundary 635.

long, *adj.* LONG 674; everlasting 670n.

gelong, *adj.* [ALONG]; *þær is help gelonʒ*, whence help comes 645.

longe, lange, *adv.* LONG, for a long time 208, 444; *(comp.)* **leng** 201, **lenge** 375n.

lufian, *w.v.(2)*, LOVE 27, 48, etc.

lufu, *f.ō-stem, later n-stem*, LOVE 31, 41, etc.

lust, *m.a-stem*, *orig. u-stem*, LUST, desire, pleasure 369, 409.

gelīfan, *w.v.(1b)*, [YLEVE]; believe 48.

lyftlācende, *pres.pt.* [LIFT + LAKE]; borne up by the air 281.

lyge, *m.i-stem*, LIE 133.

lȳtesnā, *adv.* almost 10.

JULIANA

M

mā, *comp.adv.(indec.)*, [MO]; more 413, 505; *as noun w.part.gen.* 456.

magan, *pret.pres.(5)*, MAY, can; **mæg** *(1sg.3sg.pres.)* 46, 113, etc, **meaht** *(2sg.pres.)* 53, 341, **mæge** *(opt.1sg.pres.)* 396, **meahte** *(1sg.3sg.pres.)* 392, 226, **meahtun** *(3pl.pret.)* 599*, **meahte** *(opt.1sg.3sg.pret.)* 358, 570, 572.

mān, *n.a-stem*, [MAN]; sin, evil 30, 557.

gemāna, *m.n-stem*, [YMONE]; marriage, union 127.

mānfrēa, *m.n-stem*, evil prince 546.

mānfremmende, *pres.pt.* [MAN + FREME]; doing evil 137.

mānweorc, *n.a-stem*, [MAN + WORK]; wicked deed 439, etc.

māra, *comp. adj.* MORE 36.

māþþumgesteald, *n.a-stem*, [MADME-]; treasure 36.

mǣg, *m.a-stem*, [MAY]; kinsman, fellow 528, 557.

mǣg, *f.eþ-stem*, [MAY]; maiden 175, etc.

mægden, *n.a-stem*, MAIDEN 608.

mægen, *n.a-stem*, MAIN; power, might 392, 599; host 109, etc; virtue 235; pomp 690.

mægenþrymm, *m.ja-stem*, [MAIN + THRUM]; majesty, glory, 154.

mǣglufu, *f.ō-stem, later n-stem*, [MAY + LOVE]; LOVE 70.

mǣgrǣden, *f.jō-stem*, alliance, marriage 109.

mǣgþ, *f.eþ-stem*, maiden 551, 568.

mǣgþhād, *m.a-stem, orig. u-stem*, [-HOOD]; virginity 30.

mǣlan, *w.v.(1b)*, [MELE]; speak 351, etc.

mǣlan, *w.v.(1b)*, [MEAL]; damage *(pt.p.)* 591.

mǣnan, *w.v.(1b)*, [MEAN]; lament 391, 712.

mǣne, *adj.* wicked 370.

mǣre, *adj.* [MERE]; famous, great 26, etc.

mǣst, *adj.sup.* MOST, greatest 72, 579, 659.

meaht, *f.i-stem*, MIGHT, power 182, 446, etc.

meahtig, *adj.* MIGHTY 306.

melda, *m.n-stem*, messenger 557, informer 621.

meldian, *w.v.(2)*, [MELD]; tell 463.

mengu, *f.īn-stem, later indec.*, multitude 45.

meord, *f.ō-stem*, reward 729.

meotud, *m.a-stem*, Lord 182, 306, etc.

mereflōd, *m.a-stem*, *(orig. u-stem)*, [MERE + FLOOD]; ocean 480.

(ge)mētan, *w.v.(1b)*, MEET 218*, 383, etc.

micel, *adj.* [MICKLE]; great 26, etc; *micles*, much 444; *miclum*, greatly 608; *miclan dæʒe*, Last Judgment 723.

mid, *prep.w.dat. or acc.* [MID]; with, among, by 32, 111, etc; *mid ryhte*, rightly 285; *adv.* 676.

middangeard, *m.a-stem*, [MID-DENERD]; world, earth 3, 154.

middel, *m.a-stem*, MIDDLE 568.

milde, *adj.* MILD, gentle, merciful 170, *(sup.)* 207, etc.

milts, *f.jō-stem*, [MILCE]; mercy 657.

miltsian, *w.v.(2)*, *w.dat.* [MILCE]; to have mercy 449.

mīn, *poss.adj.* MINE, my 70, 93, etc.

geminsian, *w.v.(2)*, degrade 621.

mirce, *adj.* MURK; black *(sup.)* 505.

74

misgedwield, *n.i-stem*, [MIS + I + DWILD]; evil deceit 326.

mislic, *adj.* [MISLICH]; various 406; (*w.sg. noun in pl. sense*) 363, 493.

misthelm, *m.a-stem*, [MIST + HELM]; covering of mist 470.

mōd, *n.a-stem*, MOOD; heart, mind, spirit 26, 39, etc.

mōdig, *adj.* MOODY; bold, brave 383, 513, (*as noun*) 127; noble-minded 721.

mōdlufu, *f.ō-stem, later n-stem*, [MOOD + LOVE]; affection 370, 699.

mōdsefa, *m.n-stem*, mind, heart 72, 235.

moldgræf, *n.a-stem*, [MOULD + GRAVE]; grave 690.

moldweg, *m.a-stem*, [MOULD + WAY]; (path of the) earth 334.

mon, man, 459, *m.monos-stem*, MAN 5, 84, etc.

mon, *indef.pron.* [MAN]; one 40, 578.

moncynn, *n.ja-stem*, [MANKIN]; MANkind 182, etc.

gemong, *n.a-stem*, [YMONG]; company 420, 528.

monian, *w.v.(2)*, remind 717.

monigfeald, *adj.* MANIFOLD, of many kinds 366.

monþēaw, *m.wa-stem*, [MAN + THEW]; custom 410n.

morþor, *n. or m.a-stem*, MURDER; evil 546.

*mōtan, *pret.pres.(6)*, [MOTE]; may, be allowed 518; (*w. ellipsis of verb of motion*) 457.

gemōt, *n.a-stem*, [I + MOOT]; encounter 426.

gemunan, *pret.pres.(4)*, [IMUNE, MONE]; remember 624, etc.

mundbora, *m.n-stem*, [MUND-]; protector 156, 213.

mundbyrd, *f.i-stem*, protection 170.

gemynd, *f. or n.i-stem*, MIND, thought 36.

gemyndig, *adj. w.gen.* [I + MINDY]; mindful 601.

myne, *m.i-stem*, desire 379, 657.

myrran, *w.v.(1b)*, [MAR]; lead astray (*pt.p.*) 412.

myrrelse, *f.ō-stem, later n-stem*, [MAR + -ELS]; hindrance, stumbling block 338n.

N

nabban, *see* **habban.**

nacod, *adj.* NAKED 187.

nales, nalæs 354, *adv.* not (at all) 118, 356.

nān, *pron.* NONE 514.

nāt, *see* **witan.**

nǣfre, *adv.* NEVER 55, etc.

nǣs, *see* **bēon.**

ne, *adv.* [NE]; not 33, 46, etc; *conj.* **nē,** nor 54, 135, etc; *correls.* neither...nor 591, 592.

nēah, *prep.w.dat.* [NIGH]; near 635; *adv.* near 335.

geneahhe, *adv.* very 24.

nearobregd, *n.a-stem*, [NARROW + BRAID]; evil trick 302.

genēatscolu, *f.ō-stem*, [-SHOAL]; band of retainers 684.

nemne, *conj.* unless 109.

nēod, *f.ō-stem, adv.usage* eagerly 24.

nēodful, *adj.* earnest 720.

nēol, *adj.* [NUEL]; deep 684.

nēosan, *w.v.(1b)*, *w.gen.* seek, visit 554, 631.

nergend, *m.nd-stem*, Saviour 240.

neton, *see* **witan.**

nēþan, *w.v.(1b)*, venture 302.

niht, *f.monos-stem*, NIGHT 626.

(ge)niman, *v.(4)*, [NIM]; carry off, seize 255, 288.

nīþ, *m.a-stem*, [NITH]; hatred, enmity 56, etc.

niþer, *adv*. [NETHER]; below 423.

geniþla, *m.n-stem*, foe 151.

nīþwracu, *f.ð-stem*, [NITH-WRAKE]; severe punishment 187.

nīwian, *w.v.*(2), [NEW]; renew (*pt.p.*) 607.

nōht, *n.indef.pron.* NOUGHT, nothing 329.

noma, *m.n-stem*, NAME 24, 720.

nōþ, *f.ð-stem*, daring 343.

nū, *adv.* NOW 272*, 341, etc.

nȳd, *f.i-stem*, NEED, necessity 343.

nȳdbysig, *adj.* [NEED + BUSY]; harassed by misery 423.

nȳdcleafa, *m.n-stem*, prison 240*.

nȳde, *adv.* [NEED]; of necessity 203, 462.

nyllan, *see* willan.

O

of, *prep.w.dat.* OF 333, 524; from 215,etc; beyond the reach of 215.

ofer, *prep.w.acc.* or *dat.* OVER, above 10, 432, etc; concerning 201, 444; amongst 9; on 44, etc; contrary to 23, etc.

oferhygd, *f.* or *n.i-stem*, excessive pride 424A.

oferswīðan, *w.v.*(1b), overcome 521, 543.

ofest, *f.ð-stem*, haste 253.

ofestlīce, *adv.* speedily 582.

oft, *adv.* OFT, often 12*, (*sup.*) 20n, 22, etc.

oftēon, *v.*(2), [orig.(1)]; *w.dat. and acc.* [OF + TEE]; deprive of 468

ofunnan, *pret.pres.*(3), *w.gen. and dat.* [OF + UNNE]; begrudge 377.

on, *prep.w.dat.* or *acc.* ON, in 35, 39, etc; at 163, etc; to, into, onto 6, 85, etc.; among 389.

onǣlan, *w.v.*(1b), [ANNEAL]; inflame 372, 580.

onbærnan, *w.v.*(1b), [ON + BURN]; kindle 579.

onbryrdan, *w.v.*(1b), incite 396.

oncweðan, *v.*(5), [ON + QUETHE]; reply 209, etc.

oncyrran, *w.v.*(1b), [ON + CHARE]; change, turn 144, 226, etc.

ond, *conj.* AND 9, 17, etc; if 378n.

ondettan, *w.v.*(2), confess 456*.

ondrǣdan, *v.*(7), [A DREAD]; fear 134, 210.

ondswaru, *f.ð-stem*, ANSWER 105, etc.

ondwīs, *adj.w.gen.* [AND + WISE]; skilled 244.

ongēan, *prep.w.dat.* [AGAIN]; against, towards 367, 628; *adv.* in opposition 385.

ongietan, *v.*(5), [ANGET]; know, recognize 49, 181.

ongin, *n.a-stem*, [ANGIN]; undertaking 127.

onginnan, *v.*(3), [ONGIN]; begin, set about 26, etc.; *w.auxiliary force* 290, etc.

onhātan, *v.*(7), [ON + HIGHT]; promise, vow 118, 151.

onsacan, *v.*(6), [ON + SAKE *n.* cf ATSAKE]; resist 194.

onsēcan, *w.v.*(1c), *w.gen.* [ON-SEEK]; deprive of (*p.pt.*) 679.

onsecgan, *w.v.*(3), [ON + SAY]; sacrifice 174, 199, etc.

onsendan, *w.v.*(1b), SEND (forth) 322, etc; give up 310.

onsponnan, *v.*(7), [*cf* UNSPAN]; open 79.

onsund, *adj.* [ON + SOUND]; uninjured 593, 715.

onsȳn, *f.i-stem*, [ANSIN(E)]; face 730; presence 331.

ontȳnan, *w.v.*(1b), [UNTINE]; open 402.

onwendan, *w.v.(1b)*, [AWEND]; change, turn aside 57, 144.

onwrēon, *v.(1)*, [UNWRY]; make known, declare 467, 516.

openian, *w.v.(2)*, OPEN; break open (*pt.p.*) 403.

ōr, *n.a-stem*, [ORE]; *or . . . oð ende forð*, from beginning to end 353.

ord, *m.a-stem*, [ORD]; beginning 286; spear point 471n.

orfeorme, *adj.* [OR + FARM *n.*]; worthless 217.

orlege, *n.i-stem*, hostility 97.

ormǣte, *adj.* [ORMETE]; excessive 465, 627.

orwēna, *adj.w.gen.* [OR + WEEN *n.*]; despairing of 320.

orwīge, *adj.* [OR + WI *n.*]; defenceless 434.

orwyrðu, *f.indec.* [OR + WORTH, WURTHE, *adj.*]; dishonour 69.

oð, *prep.w.acc.* until 694; to (*see* ōr) 353.

oðcyrran, *w.v.(1b)*, [-CHARE]; change, be perverted 338*.

ōþer, *pron.* and *adj.* OTHER, another 75, etc.

oþþæt, *conj.* until 285.

oþþe, *conj.* [OTHER]; or 77, etc; *correls.* either...or 335.

oðþringan, *v.(3)*, [-THRING]; *w. dat. and acc.* take away by force 500.

ōwer, *adv.* [OWHERE]; anywhere 331.

R

gerǣcan, *w.v.(1c)*, [I + REACH]; attack 73, 300.

rǣd, *m.a-stem*, [REDE]; advice 99.

rǣran, *w.v.(1b)*, REAR; wage 12, etc.; exalt 48.

rǣs, *m.i-stem*, [RESE]; onslaught 587.

recene, *adv.* [REKEN *adj.*]; quickly 62.

gerēfa, *m.n-stem*, REEVE; *senator* 19, 530.

rēonig, *adj.* dark, gloomy 481n*, 530.

reord, *f.ō-stem*, [RERD(E)]; voice, speech 62.

reordian, *w.v.(2)*, [RERD(E)]; speak 66.

restan, *w.v.(1b)*, REST, cease 200.

rēþe, *adj.* [RETHE]; fierce 140; stern 704.

rīce, *n.ja-stem*, [RICHE]; kingdom 8, 66.

rīce, *adj.* RICH, powerful 19.

rīm, *n.a-stem*, [RIME]; number 587; large number 368.

gerīm, *n.a-stem*, [I + RIME]; number 314.

rīman, *w.v.(1b)*, [RIME]; recount 505.

rōd, *f.ō-stem*, ROOD; cross 305, etc.

rodor, *m.a-stem*, firmament 498; heaven 305, 644.

rodorcyning, *m.a-stem*, KING of heaven 447.

rondburg, *f.monos-stem*, [RAND + BOROUGH]; (fortified) town 19.

rūme, *adv.* [ROOM]; in full 314.

rūn, *f.ō-stem*, [ROUN]; counsel 62; mystery 656.

ryht, *n.a-stem*, RIGHT; *mid ryhte*, truthfully 285.

ryhtfremmende, *pres.pt.* [RIGHT + FREME]; righteous 8.

ryne, *m.i-stem*, [RUNE]; course 498.

S

sacan, *v.(6)*, [SAKE *n.*]; strive, contend 206, 298.

sacu, *f.ō-stem*, [SAKE]; strife, dispute 200, 230.

sār, *n.a-stem*, SORE; suffering, torment 55, etc.

sārlīce, *adv.* SORELY, painfully (*sup.*) 571.

sārslege,*m.i-stem*, [SORE + SLAY]; painful blow 341, 547.

sārwracu, *f.ō-stem*, [SORE + WRACK]; grievous suffering or punishment 527.

sāwul, sāwl 669, *f.ō-stem*, SOUL 348, etc.

sǣmra, *comp.adj.* inferior, worse 51, 361.

sǣne, *adj.* (*comp.*) less active 395.

scamu, *f.ō-stem*, SHAME 445.

sceacan, *v.*(6), [SHAKE]; *on fleam sceacan*, take to flight 630.

gesceaft, *f. or n.i-stem*, [I + SHAFT]; creation 562; creature 183; decree 728n.

gesceap, *n.a-stem*, [I + SHAPE]; creation 273.

sceaþa, *m.n-stem*, [SCATHE]; evildoer, enemy 672.

scēohmōd, *adj.* [SHY + MOOD]; fearful (wanton?) of heart 672.

sceþþan, *v.*(6) *or w.v.*(1a),*w.dat.* [SCATHE]; injure 349.

gescieppan, *v.*(6), [I + SHAPE] create 111.

scīma, *m.n-stem*,[*see* SHIM: shadow, SHIM *adj.*]; brightness, splendour 166.

scinlāc, *n.a-stem*, [-LAKE]; delusion, rage 214.

scip, *n.a-stem*, SHIP 672.

scīr, *adj.* [SHIRE]; glorious 728n.

gescomian, *w.v.*(2), *w.gen.* [I + SHAME]; to be ashamed of 713.

scræf, *n.a-stem*, pit 684.

scrīfan, *v.*(1), [SHRIVE]; decree 728.

scūfan, *v.*(2), SHOVE, thrust 584.

sculan, *pret.pres.*(4), SHALL, must, should; **sceal** (*1sg.3sg.pres.*) 115, 203, etc; (*w. ellipsis of verb of motion*) 699; **scealt** (*2sg.pres.*) 256, etc; **sceolan** (*3pl.pres.*) 195;

sceolde (*3sg.pret.*) 611; **sceolde** (*1sg.2sg.pret.subj.*) 425, 524.

scūr, *m.a-stem*, SHOWER; cloud 472; beating rain 651.

scyld, *f.i-stem*, [SHILDY *adj.*]; guilt 584.

scyld, *m.a-stem*, *orig. u-stem*, SHIELD 386.

gescyldan, *w.v.*(1b), [I + SHIELD]; protect 214.

scyldig, *adj.w.dat.* [SHILDY]; forfeit of 124.

scyldwyrcende, *pres.pt.* [SHILDY *adj.* + WORK]; committing sin 445.

scyndan, *w.v.*(1b), [SKIND]; hasten forth 489.

scyppend, *m.nd-stem*, [SHEPPEND]; creator 181.

sē, *dem.pron.* he, she, it, this; *m.nom.sg.* 580; **sēo**, *f.nom.sg.* 258; **þæt**, *n.nom.sg.* 545; **þone**, *m.acc.sg* 111; **þæt**, *n.acc.sg.* 1, etc; **þām**, *m. and n.dat.sg.* 377, etc; **þā**, *nom.pl.* 216; *acc.pl.* 122; **þāra**, *gen.pl.* 510, 518; **þȳ, þī** 556, *instr.w.comp.* the 355, etc; *w.* **lǣs** 649, 664; **þon**, *instr. see* **ǣr**; *w.* **þē** *to form rel.* **sē**, *nom.sg.* 415, 447; **þāra**, *gen.pl.* 207, 354, etc.

sē, *rel.pron.* who, which; *nom.sg.* 3, etc; **þone**, *acc.sg.* 616; **þæs**, *gen.sg.* 182; **þā**, *nom. and acc.pl.* 13, 490, etc; **þām**, *dat.pl.* 500.

sē, *def.art.* the; *nom.sg.* 38, etc, **þone**, *acc.sg.* 284, etc.; **þæs**, *gen.sg.* 37, etc.; **þām**,*dat.sg.* 225, etc; **sēo, sīo** 32, *f.nom.sg.* 93; etc; **þā**, *f.acc.sg.* 114, etc; **þǣre**, *f.gen.sg.* 59, etc; *f.dat.sg.* 21 etc; **þæt**, *n.nom.sg.* 36, etc, *n.acc.sg.* 45, etc; **þæs**, *n.gen.sg.* 583, etc; **þām**, *n.dat.sg.* 184, etc; **þȳ**, *m.instr.* 587; **þā**, *nom.pl.* 71;

78

etc; *acc.pl.* 75, etc; **þǣre**, *gen.pl.* 38n; **þām**, *dat.pl.* 152.

searoþonc, *m.a-stem*, [-THANK]; *dat.pl.* cunningly 298, 494.

sēaŏ, *m.a-stem*, *orig. u-stem*, [SEATH]; pit 413, 422.

(ge)sēcan, *w.v.(1c)*, SEEK, look for 116, etc; resort to 23; go, go to 424, etc; *p.pt.* assailed with 490, enveloped in 624n.

secg, *m.ja-stem*, [SEGGE]; man 676.

(ge)secgan, *w.v.(3)*, SAY, tell 46, etc.

sefa, *m.n-stem*, mind, heart 94, 342.

sēlla, *adj.comp.* [*cf* SELE *pos.*]; better 407; **sēlestan** (*sup.*) best 206.

sellend, syllend 705, *m.nd-stem*, SELL *v.*; giver 668.

semninga, *adv.* suddenly 242, 614.

sendan, *w.v.(1b)*, SEND 262, etc.

sēoc, *adj.* SICK, afflicted 65.

seofian, *w.v.(2)*, lament 537.

seomian, *w.v.(2)*, lie 709.

sēon, *v.(5)*, SEE; *w. to*, look on, gaze 291.

settan, *w.v.(1a)*, *orig.* (1c), SET, establish 274.

gesettan, *w.v.(1a)*, *orig.* (1c), [ISET]; make, bring about (peace) 200.

sibb, *f.jō-stem*, [SIB]; peace 200, etc; kindness 219; bond 698.

sīd, *adj.* [SIDE]; wide 332.

sīdfolc, *n.a-stem*, [SIDE + FOLK]; multitude 692n.

siex, *num.* SIX 230.

sigor, *m.a-stem*, *orig. -os-es-stem* (Sievers §289, 2, n. 5), victory, triumph 224, etc.

sigortifer, *n.a-stem*, sacrifice for deliverance 255n*.

singāl, *adj.* constant 242.

singrim, *adj.* [SEN (*as in* SEN-GREEN) + GRIM]; unceasingly fierce 230.

sinhīwan, *m.n-stem*, *pl.* united pair 698.

sinige, *f.n-stem*, companion, wife 54n*.

gesittan, *v.(5)*, SIT 495.

sīþ, *m.a-stem*, [SITHE]; undertaking, errand 443, etc; time 354n*.

gesīŏ, *m.a-stem*, companion 242.

sīþ, *adj.* (*sup.*) last 475.

sīþ, *adv.* 496, 548, 710 (*see* ǣr).

sīþfæt, *m.a-stem*, [SITHE]; journey, undertaking, errand 285, 318, etc.

sīþian, *w.v.(2)*, [SITHE]; journey (*pres.pt.*) 261, 714.

sīþþan, *conj.* [SITHEN]; after, since 63, etc; *adv.* afterwards 330, etc.

slēan, *v.(6)*, SLAY, smite 494.

slege, *m.i-stem*, [SLAY]; stroke, blow 229.

slide, *m.i-stem*, falling 349.

snell, *adj.* [SNELL]; swift 60.

snotor, *adj.* [SNOTER]; *sup.* wise 543.

sōna, *adv.* SOON; immediately 49, etc.

sorg, *f.ō-stem*, SORROW, affliction 443, etc.

sorgcearig, *adj.* [SORROW + CHARY]; sorrowful, wretched 603, 709.

sorgstæf, *m.a-stem*, [SORROW + STAFF]; trouble 660.

sōŏ, *n.a-stem*, [SOOTH]; truth 342; *to soŏe*, truly 132, 547.

sōŏ, *adj.* [SOOTH]; true 42, etc.

sōŏfæst, *adj.* [SOOTHFAST]; righteous 325, etc.

sōŏlice, *adv.* [SOOTHLY]; truly 561.

sparian, *w.v.(2)*, SPARE, show mercy 85.

spild, *m.i-stem*, destruction 85.

spīowian, *w.v.(2)* *orig.* (1b), (Sievers § 408, n. 13 and 15); SPEW; *w.dat.* spurt 476.

spor, *n.a-stem*; *pæpnes spor*, wound 623.

spræc, *f.jō-stem*, SPEECH, discussion 89, 533.

(ge)sprecan, *v.(5)*, SPEAK 145, 185, etc.

springan, *v.(3)*, SPRING, burst out 585.

stān, *m.a-stem*, STONE; rock 654.

staþelian, *w.v.(2)*, [STATHEL]; make steadfast (*p.pt.*) 107, etc.

staþol, *m.a-stem*, [STADDLE]; foundation 654.

staþolfæst, *adj.* [STADDLE + FAST]; firm 374.

stearc, *adj.* STARK; rough 282.

stearcferþ, *adj.* cruel 636

stefn, *f.ō-stem*, [STEVEN]; voice 282.

steppan, *v.(6)*, STEP; advance 374.

stihtend, *m.nd-stem*, [STIGHT v.]; ruler 419.

stīðhydig, *adj.* [STITH-]; resolute 654n.

stondan, *v.(6)*, STAND 277, etc; be 123.

storm, *m.a-stem*, STORM 651.

stōw, *f.wō-stem*, [STOW]; place 636.

strēam, *m.a-stem*, STREAM; water, sea 481.

strong, *adj.* STRONG, firm 651; hard, severe 464.

stronglīce, *adv.* STRONGLY; boldly, 374.

stӯran, *w.v.* (*1b*), STEER; rebuke 296.

sum, *indef.pron.* SOME 472, etc; a certain one 18.

sumerlong, *adj.* [SUMMER + LONG]; live-long 495n.

gesund, *adj.* [ISOUND]; sound, unhurt 568.

sunne, *f.n-stem*, SUN 166.

sunsciene, *adj.* [SUN + SHEEN]; radiant as the sun 229A.

sunu, *m.u-stem*, SON 725.

sūsl, *n.a-stem*, or *f.ō-stem*, torment 142, etc.

swā, *adv. conj.* so 73, etc; exceedingly 170; likewise 504; *conj.* as, 11, 81, etc; when 253; *swa . . . swa*, or . . . just as 88.

sweart, *adj.* SWART; dark, black 313, etc.

sweltan, *v.(3)*, [SWELT]; die 125.

swencan, *w.v.(1b)*, [SWENCHE]; trouble 47.

sweopu, *see* swipu.

swēor, *m.a-stem*, father-in-law 65, 78n*.

gesweorcan, *v.(3)*, [1 + SWERK]; become angry 78.

sweordbite, *m.i-stem*, [SWORD + BIT]; sword wound 603.

sweordgripe, *m.i-stem*, [SWORD + GRIP]; seizing of swords 488.

sweordslege, *m.i-stem*, [SWORD + SLAY]; sword stroke 671.

sweotolīce, *adv.* [SUTEL + LY]; plainly (*comp.*) 355.

sweotul, *adj.* [SUTEL]; plain, clear 551.

geswerian, *v.(6)*, SWEAR 80.

(ge)swētan, *w.v.(1b)*, SWEET; sweeten, make pleasant 369, 525.

swēte, *adj.* SWEET, charming *sup.* 94, 166.

(ge)swīcan, *v.(1)*, [SWIKE]; cease 373; be a traitor to (*w.dat.*) 387; *w.gen.* cease from 120.

swingan, *v.(3)*, SWING, SWINGE; scourge, beat 142, 188; afflict 337, 617.

swipu, *f.n-stem*, [SWEPE]; scourge, rod 188.

swīþe, *adv.* [SWITH]; much, greatly 99, etc; *comp.* farther 47; *sup.* especially, very greatly 349, 620.

swīðferð, *adj.* [SWITH-]; violent of mind 78.

swĭðlic, *adj.* [SWITHLY *adv.*]; severe 55.

swonrād, *f.ð-stem,* [SWAN+ROAD]; sea 675.

swylc, *adj.* SUCH 426.

swylce, *adv.* [SUCH]; likewise 51, etc.

swylt, *m.i-stem,* death 255, 675.

sylf, *pron.* SELF, own 46, 99, etc.

syllan, *w.v.(1c),* SELL; give 289, 522.

symle, *adv.* always 20n, 238, 669.

syn, *f.jō-stem,* SIN 65, 188, etc.

sȳn, *f.i-stem,* [SENE]; power of sight 468.

gesȳne, *adj.* [(Y)SENE]; seen 475.

synscaþa, *m.n-stem,* [SIN + SCATHE]; miscreant 671.

gesyrwan, *w.v.(1b),* devise, plot 468.

T

tācen, *n.a-stem,* TOKEN; Sign of the Cross 491.

tǣl, *f.i-stem,* [TELE]; blasphemy 73.

tǣlan, *w.v.(1b),* [TELE]; blaspheme 598.

tǣlnis, *f.jō-stem,* [TELE + NESS]; blasphemy 205.

tēar, *m.a-stem,* TEAR 712.

tellan, *w.v.(1c),* TELL; consider 357.

(ge)teohhian, tiohhian 215, *w.v.(2),* consider 215; decree (*p.pt.*) 264.

(ge)tēon, *v.(2),* [TEE]; drag 534; *ʒewin tuʒe,* brought about strife, 421; incite 483.

tēona, *m.n-stem,* [TEEN]; iniquity 402, 458.

tēoncwide, *m.i-stem,* [TEEN + QUIDE]; blasphemy 205.

teran, *v.(4),* TEAR, rend 595.

tīd, *f.i-stem,* TIDE; hour 230, 712; time 724, 731.

tiohhian, *see* teohhian.

tō, *adv.* TOO 99, etc; *prep.w.dat.* TO, for, from 41, etc; *w.inf.* 408, etc; *þe, me to gewealde,* into thy, my, power 87, 412; at (*w.obj. omitted*) 291.

tōgædre, *adv.* TOGETHER 63.

tōlȳsan, *w.v.(1b),* [TO + LEESE]; set free (*p.pt.*) 585.

torn, *adj.* grievous 205.

torne, *adv.* grievously 73.

torr, *m.a-stem,* TOWER 402.

tōscādan, *v.(7),* [TOSHED]; separate (*p.pt.*) 584.

tōscūfan, *v.(2),* [TO + SHOVE]; thrust aside 564.

tōslītan, *v.(1),* [TO + SLITE]; tear apart, sever 698.

tōweorpan, *v.(3),* [TOWARP]; scatter 566; throw down 650.

trēo, *n.wa-stem,* TREE 447.

trēow, *f.wō-stem,* TRUCE (*orig. pl. form*); faith 29, 655.

getrēowan, *w.v.(1b),* *orig.* (2), [I + TROW]; trust 435.

trum, *adj.* [TRIM, (UN)TRUM]; firm (*comp.*) 650.

trymman, *w.v.(1a),* [TRIM; encourage 638.

tū, *see* twēgen.

tūdor, *n.a-stem,* [TUDDER]; children 459.

tungol, *n.a-stem,* star 498.

twēgen, *num.* [TWAIN]; two 698.

þ

þā, *adv.* [THO]; then 26, etc; *nu þa,* now 511, 520; *conj.* when 146, etc.

þafian, *w.v.(2),* [THAVE]; consent to 108, 126; endure, submit to 466.

þær, *adv.* THERE 218, etc; *conj.* where 91, etc; when 302, 452; if 570n.

þæs, *adv.* [THES]; such, to such a degree, so 55, 103, etc.

þæs þe, *conj.* because 599.

þæt, *conj.* THAT 30, etc; because 621; so that 292, etc; when 691.

þætte, *conj.* which 2.

þē, *indec.rel.pron.* [THE]; who, which, that 37, etc; *see* sē, *dem.pron.*

þēah, *conj.* THOUGH, although 192, etc.

þēah þe, *conj.* although 42, 515.

þearf, *f.ō-stem,* [THARF]; need 659, etc.

þearlic, *adj.* severe 678.

þegn, *m.a-stem,* THANE, man, warrior, follower, servant 12,152, etc.

þencan, *w.v.(1c),* [THENCHE]; THINK, purpose 637.

þenden, *conj.* whilst 714.

þennan, *w.v.(1a),* [THIN]; stretch out 187.

þēoden, *m.a-stem,* lord, chief 82, etc, prince 524.

þēodscipe, *m.i-stem,* [THEDE + SHIP]; friendship 178; people (due observance?) 695.

þēon, *v.(1), later (2),* [THEE]; *w.dat* profit 605.

þēs, *dem.adj.m.* THIS 208, etc; þisne, *m.acc.sg.* 527, 694; þissum, *m.dat.sg.* 701; þēos, *f.nom.sg.* 464; þās, *f.acc.sg.* 321; þisse, *f.dat.sg.* 343; þis, *n.nom. and acc.sg.* 190, 201, etc; þissum, *n.dat.sg.* 74; þās, *nom.pl.* 83; þissa, *gen.pl.* 57.

þicgan, *v.(5),* [THIG]; receive 687.

þīn, *poss.pron.* THINE, thy 50, 68, etc.

þing, *n.a-stem,* THING 465.

(ge)þingian, *w.v.(2),* [THING]; address (*w.pið*) 260, 429; to be reconciled to 198; intercede 717.

þingrǣden, *f.jō-stem,* proposal of marriage 126.

geþōht, *m. or n.a-stem,* THOUGHT, purpose 550.

(ge)þolian, *w.v.(2),* [THOLE]; suffer, endure, undergo 340n., 464, etc.

þonan, *adv.* [THENNE]; thence 384, 389.

þonc, *m.a-stem,* [THANK]; *secgan þonc,* give thanks 593.

geþonc, *m.a-stem,* [ITHANK]; thought 358n, etc.

þoncwyrþe, *adj.* [THANK + WURTHE]; acceptable 198.

þonne, *adv.* THEN 203, etc; therefore 715.

þonne, *conj.* THAN 36, etc; when 325, etc.

þracu, *f.ō-stem,* violence 12, 333.

þrāg, *f.ō-stem,* [THROW]; time (of distress) 453, 464.

þrāgmǣl, *n.a-stem,* [THROW + MEAL]; unhappy time 344A.

þrǣchwīl, *f.ō-stem,* time of suffering 554.

þrēa, *f.wō-stem or m.n-stem,* punishment, misery 520, 678.

þrēagan, *w.v.(2),* orig. *w.v.(3),* [THREA]; torture, afflict 142, (*p.pt.*) 344; chastise 546.

þrēanēd, *f.i-stem,* [-NEED]; punishing affliction 464.

þrēanīedlic, *adj.w.dat.* calamitous 128*.

þrēat, *m.a-stem,* THREAT; troop 672; punishment 465.

geþrēatian, *w.v.(2),* [I + THREAT]; bring about by threatening 54, 176.

þriste, *adj.* [THRISTE]; bold (*comp.*) 550; audacious 358.

þriste, *adv.* boldly 511.

þrittig, *num.* THIRTY 678. (MS XXX.)

(ge)þrōwian, *w.v.(2),* [THROW]; suffer 229, etc.

þrymm, *m.ja-stem*, [THRUM]; glory, majesty 280, 448; (of God) 641; splendour (*or* host?) 694.

þrymsittende, *pres.pt.* [THRUM + SITTING]; dwelling in glory 435, 726.

þrýnes, *f.jō-stem*, [THRINNESS]; Trinity 726.

þrýþful, *adj.* powerful 12.

þū, *pron.* THOU, you 46, etc; þec, þé, *acc.sg.* 46, etc; þé, *dat.sg.* 46, etc.

geþungen, *adj.*(*p.pt. of* þeon), noble 262.

*þurfan, *pret.pres.*(3), [THARF]; need, have reason 46, etc.

þurh, *prep.w.acc.* THROUGH, by reason of, by, in 14, 52, etc.

þurhtéon, *v.*(2), [THROUGH + TEE]; accomplish (*pt.p.*) 458.

þus, *adv.* THUS, in this manner, to this extent 311, 362, etc.

þweorhtimber, *adj.* [THWART]; + TIMBER *n.*]; resolutely made (*comp.*) 550n.

þý, *adv.* [THY]; by this means 256.

geþýdan, *w.v.*(1b), associate 419.

þyncan, *w.v.*(1c), *impers.w.dat.* [THINK]; seem, appear 87, etc.

þyrel, *adj.* [THIRL *n.*]; pierced 402.

þyslic, *adj.* [THELLICH]; such 453.

þýstre, *adj.* [THESTER]; dark, gloomy 419, 683.

þýstru, *f.īn-stem, later indec.,* [THESTER]; darkness 333, etc.

U

ufan, *adv.* [*cf* ABOVE]; from above 261.

unbeald, *adj.* [UNBOLD]; *comp.* less bold 423.

unbiþyrfe, *adj.* [UN + BE + THARF *v.*]; vain, unprofitable 97, 217.

unbrice, *adj.* [UN + BRUCHE *n.*]; inviolate, unshaken 235.

uncer, *poss.pron.* [UNKER]; our 190.

uncláne, *adj.* UNCLEAN 418.

uncýþu, *f.indec.orig.ō-stem,* [UN + KITH]; ignorance 701n.

under, *prep.w.acc. or dat.* UNDER, within, in 43, etc.

unforht, *adj.* fearless 209, 601; *as noun* 147.

ungéara, *adv.* [UN + YORE]; soon 124.

ungebletsod, *p.pt.* UNBLESSED 492.

ungelíce, *adv.* [UNILECHE]; in different manner 688.

ungewemmed, *adj.* [UNWEMMED]; uninjured 590.

unláed, *adj.* [UNLEDE]; wretched 616.

unmáete, *adj.* [UNMEET]; boundless 517.

unnan, *pret. pres.*(3), *w.gen. and dat.* [UNNE]; grant 192.

unráed, *m.a-stem,* [UNREDE]; ill-advised course 120.

unrim, *n.a-stem, w.part.gen.* [UN + RIME]; countless 43, etc.

unryht, *adj.* [UNRIGHT]; unlawful 297.

unsáelig, *adj.* [UNSEELY]; miserable 450.

unscamig, *adj.* [UN + SHAME *n.*]; unconfounded 552.

unsnytru, unsnyttru 145, *f.ō-stem, orig. n-stem, dat.pl.* foolishly 145, 308.

unwáclíce, *adv.* [UN + WOKELY]; resolutely 50.

unwáerlic, *adj.* [UN + WARELY]; incautious 193.

ūp, *adv.* UP 62, 644.

ūser, *poss.pron.* OUR 129, etc.

ūt, *adv.* OUT 253, 532.

ūtgong, *m.a-stem,* [OUTGANG]; departure 661.

W

wā, *interj.w.dat.* WOE 632.

wæccan, *w.v.(3)*, [WECCHE]; be vigilant (*pres.pt.*) 662.

wāflan, *w.v.(2)*, to look with amazement 162.

waldend, *m.nd-stem*, [WALDEND]; Lord 213, etc.

wānian, *w.v.(2)*, [WONE]; lament 538.

wǣg, wēg 479n*, *m.i-stem*, [WAW]; wave 680.

wǣgan, *w.v.(1b)*, afflict 143.

wǣpen, *n.a-stem*, WEAPON 623.

wǣr, *adj.w.gen.* WARE; cautious (*comp.*) 425.

wǣrfæst, *adj.* [WARE + FAST]; faithful 238.

wǣrlēas, *adj.* [WARE + LESS]; faithless 351, 421.

wǣrlic, *adj.* [WARELY]; prudent 662.

wǣrloga, *m.n-stem*, [WARLOCK]; traitor, devil 455.

wæs, *see* bēon.

wæter, *n.a-stem*, WATER 292, 479.

wē, *pron.* WE 1, etc; ūsic, *acc.pl.* 325, 336; ūs, *dat.pl.* 122, etc.

weal, *m.a-stem*, WALL 401, 650.

geweald, *n.a-stem*, [1 + WIELD]; power 86*, etc.

wealdan, *v.(7)*, *w.gen.dat. or prep.* WIELD, rule, have dominion over 19, etc.

weallan, *v.(7)*, [WALL]; boil, surge 581.

weard, *m.a-stem*, [WARD]; guardian 212.

weard, *f.ō-stem*, WARD; watch 664.

weardian, *w.v.(2)*, [WARD]; inhabit 20, 92.

wēdan, *w.v.(1b)*, [WEDE]; rage 597.

weg, *m.a-stem*, WAY, path 282, etc.

wēge, *n.ja-stem*, cup 487.

wela, *m.n-stem*, [WEAL]; riches (*or* abundantly) 76.

welgrim, *adj.* [WAL + GRIM]; cruel 264.

welig, *adj.* [WEALY]; rich (*as noun*) 33, etc.

wēn, *f.i-stem*, [WEEN]; probability 632.

wēnan, *w.v.(1b)*, [WEEN]; suppose, believe 357, 425; *w.gen.* expect 453, 686.

wendan, *w.v.(1b)*, [WEND]; change 570.

wēoh, *m.a-stem*, idol 23.

wēohweorðing, *f.ō-stem*, [-WORTH + ING]; sacrifice 180.

weorc, *n.a-stem*, WORK 560*; distress 569; *dat. w.* bēon, to be painful to 72, 135.

geweorc, *n.a-stem*, WORK 237.

weorþ, *adj.w.dat.* WORTH; precious (*sup.*) 248.

(ge)weorþan, *v.(3)*, [WORTH]; be, become 58, 156, etc; (*w.dat.*) befall 197, 503, etc.

weorþian, *w.v.(2)*, [WORTH]; show honour to, worship 76, 153.

weorðlic, *adj.* [WORTHLY]; splendid 9.

weorud, *n.a-stem*, [WERED]; multitude 291; host 515; people 647.

wer, *m.a-stem*, [WERE]; man 45, etc.

werig (werge, Klaeber n. to l. 133), *adj.* [WARY n.]; accursed (*as noun*) 429.

werþēod, *f.ō-stem*, [WERE + THEDE]; people, nation 9, etc.

wīc, *n.a-stem*, [WICK]; dwelling place 92.

wīd, *adj.* WIDE, spacious 9; *widan feore*, for ever 508n.

wīde, *adv.* WIDE; far and wide 585.

wīdeferh, -ferg 467, *n. or m.a-stem*, *acc.sg.* for a long time 223.

wīf, *n.a-stem*, WIFE; woman 432, etc.

wīfgiftu, *n.i-stem pl.orig.f.* [WIFE + GIFT]; marriage 38n.

wīflufu, *f.n-stem*, *orig. ō-stem*, [WIFE + LOVE]; love for a woman 296.

wīg, *n.a-stem*, [WI]; battle 576.

wīga, *m.n-stem*, [WYE]; warrior, man 641, 680.

wīgþrist, *adj.* [WI + THRISTE]; bold in fight 432.

wilde, *adj.* WILD 597.

willa, *m.n-stem*, WILL, purpose, desire 32, 50, etc.

willan, *anom.v.* WILL 108, etc; nyllan, *neg.* [NILL], 126, etc.

gewin, gewyn, 190, *n.a-stem*, [IWIN]; strife, struggle 421.

winburg, *f.monos-stem*, [WINE + BOROUGH]; town of feasting 83A.

wind, *m.a-stem*, WIND 650.

gewindæg, *m.a-stem*, [IWIN + DAY]; day of trouble 611.

gewinna, *m.n-stem*, enemy 243, 345, 555n*.

winnan, *v.(3)*, WIN; contend 421.

winsele, *m.i-stem*, [WINE + SEL (*as in* LEVESEL)]; hall of feasting 487, 686.

wīsdōm, *m.a-stem*, WISDOM 516.

wīse, *f.n-stem*, [WISE]; course 98.

gewit, *n.ja-stem*, [IWIT]; mind 144, 597.

wita, *m.n-stem*, [WITE]; wise man 98.

witan, *pret.pres.(1)*, [WIT]; know 91, etc: nāt, neton, *neg.* [NOT], 660, 700.

wīte, *n.ja-stem*, [WITE]; punishment, torment 56, 143, etc.,

wītebrōga, *m.n-stem*, fearful torment 135, 196.

wītga, *m.n-stem*, [WITIE]; prophet 515.

witod, *adj.* certain 357; allotted 686.

wið, *prep.w.acc. or dat.* WITH, from, against 67, 141, etc; *adv.* see þingian.

wiþerbreca, *m.n-stem*, [WITHER-]; adversary 269.

wiþerfeohtend, *m.nd-stem*, [WITHER + FIGHT]; foe 664.

wiþerhycgende, *pres.pt.* [WITHER + HOWE, HIGH *n.*]; having antagonistic thoughts 196*.

wiþersteall, *m.a-stem*, [WITHER + STALL]; defences 401n*, 441.

wiðgongan, *v.(7)*, [WITH + GANG]; overcome 393.

wiðhycgan, *w.v.(3)*, [*see* **wiþerhycgende**]; to be resolute against 42.

wiðsacan, *v.(6), w.dat.* [WITHSAKE]; refuse 99; renounce 361.

wiðstondan, *v.(6)*, *w.dat. and gen.* WITHSTAND, resist, obstruct 427, etc.

wlite, *m.i-stem*, [WLITE]; beauty of form or countenance 163, etc.

wlitescȳne, *adj.* [WLITE + SHEEN]; beautiful 454.

wlitig, *adj.* [WLITI (*under* WLITE)]; glorious 283.

wlōh, *f.monos.-stem*, [WLO]; hem 590.

wolcen, *n.a-stem*, WELKIN; *pl.* heavens 283.

wōma, *m.n-stem*, sound of terror 576A.

womdǣd, *f.i-stem*, [WAM, WEM + DEED]; evil deed 467.

womsceaða, *m.n-stem*, [WAM, WEM + SCATHE]; evildoer 211.

wōpig, *adj.* [WOPI (*under* WOP)]; mournful 711.

word, *n.a-stem*, WORD, speech, words 23, 45, etc.

woruld, *f.ō-stem*, WORLD 416, etc.

woruldrīce, *n.ja-stem*, [WORLD + RICHE]; kingdom of this world 549.

wrāð, *adj.* WROTH; cruel, fierce 177, 311; evil 507.

wrāþe, *adv.* [WROTHE]; cruelly 172.

wrǣcca, *m.n-stem*, WRETCH; exile 351.

wrǣcmæcga, *m.n-stem*, [WRACK-]; wretch 260.

wrecan, *v.(5)*, WREAK; avenge 204, 623; recite 719.

wrōht, *m.a-stem* (*f.ō-stem*), sin, crime 346, etc.

wudubēam, *m.a-stem*, [WOOD + BEAM]; forest tree 576.

wuldor, *n.a-stem* [WULDER]; glory 153, etc.

wuldorcyning, *m.a-stem*, [WULDER + KING]; king of glory 238, etc.

wund, *f.ō-stem*, WOUND, 355, 710.

wundian, *w.v.(2)*, WOUND 291.

wundor, *n.a-stem*, WONDER; *dat. pl.* wondrously 264.

wundorcrǣft, *m.i-stem*, [WONDER + CRAFT]; wondrous skill, 575.

(ge)wunian, *w.v.(2)*, [WON]; remain 238; be 37; remain (steadfast) 375.

wylm, *m.i-stem*, [WALM]; surge, gushing 478, etc.

wyn, *f.i-* or *jō-stem*, [WIN]; joy 641, 730.

wyrcan, *w.v.(1c)*, WORK 541.

gewyrcan, *w.v.(1c)*, [IWURCHE]; commit 711; construct (*pt.p.*) 401; carry out (*pt.p.*) 172n.

wyrd, *f.i-stem*, WEIRD; lot, fate 33, 538A.

gewyrht, *f. or n.i-stem*, [IWURHT]; deed 728.

wyrhta, *m.n-stem*, WRIGHT; *wrohtes wyrhta*, evildoer 346.

wyrm, *m.i-stem*, WORM, 416.

wyrrest, *adj. sup.* WORST 152, etc.

wyrþe, *adj.w.gen.* [WURTHE]; worthy of, 103, 643.

Y

yfel, *n.a-stem*, EVIL 244, etc.

yfel, *adj.* EVIL, grievous 634.

yfeldǣd, *f.i-stem*, EVIL DEED 456, 713.

yfelþweorg, *adj.* [EVIL + THWART (from O.N. cognate)]; wickedly antagonistic 90n*.

ymb, *prep.w.acc.* [UMBE, EMBE]; concerning 414.

ymbberan, *v.(4)*, [UMBE + BEAR]; surround (*p.pt.*) 581.

ymbhwyrft, *m.i-stem*, circuit, regions 113.

yrmen, *adj.* spacious 10.

yrmþu, *f.ō-stem*, later indec. [ERMTHE(E)]; misery 504, 634.

yrre, *adj.* [IRRE]; angry 140.

yrre, *n.ja-stem*, [IRRE]; anger 58, etc.

ȳþfaru, *f.ō-stem*, [YTHE + FARE]; waves, sea 478.

ȳwan, *w.v.(1b)*, show (*pt.p.*) 69.

INDEX OF PROPER NAMES

APPENDIX

WORDS OF PROBLEMATICAL MEANING

æpplede 688. There is no need to postulate a verb *æpplian*
with Strunk, since the ending here is probably the adjectival
suffix, as distinct from the p.pt. (cf NED ed², and Wright
§ 624.) This epithet occurs twice elsewhere: *Elene* 1259 and
Phoenix 506, in both of which contexts, as in this one, it is
descriptive of gold. According to the NED the noun apple is
used of 'anything resembling an apple in form or colour'. For
such usages in OE cf *irenum aplum* (*Solomon and Saturn* 28 B):
'iron balls', and the compound *æppelfealuwe* (*Beowulf* 2165):
'bay'. If the comparison lies in the colour, this phrase is equivalent to *read gold* (cf *Daniel* 59) as opposed to *geolo gold*; if the
comparison lies in the shape, however, the best meaning for the
word would be 'round'. The difficulty in the latter, however, lies
in the fact that whilst the use of *æppel* for a globe-shaped object
is authenticated, there is no other instance in English of its
being used of things which are merely circular, such as rings,
etc. *Æppel* is used of the pupil of the eye, which suggests that it
could also refer to semi-spherical objects such as bosses (BT
accept this interpretation). But whilst the boss was undoubtedly
a form of ornamentation on jewellery, as the Desborough neck-
lace and the Sutton Hoo buckle testify, it seems unlikely that
such elaborate objects would form a common part of the treasure
usually dispensed by a lord to his retainers—the *Brosinga mene*
in *Beowulf* l. 1199 is regarded as an exceptional gift—and
this type of treasure is clearly referred to in all three occurrences of the phrase (in *Juliana* it would in fact appear to
be a synonymous variant of *beagas*). Some association with
the later 'dapple-grey' seems inescapable, but the meaning of
the latter is so uncertain ('streaked like an apple', 'spotted
like a pool', etc. cf NED s.v. dapple-grey), and its relation to
ON *apalgrar*, OHG *aphelgra*, etc. so unclear, that it does not
elucidate the OE meaning. Miss Gradon in her note to *Elene*
1259 argues persuasively for 'round' and the contexts certainly
favour this interpretation. Mr Blake in his note to *Phoenix* 506
prefers 'streaked'.

cearȝealdor 618. This is a nonce word, probably an ordinary variant of *hearmleoð* 615. It does remain possible, however, that *ȝealdor* retains here its usual meaning of incantation or charm. cf L. L. Schücking 'Das angelsächsische Totenklagelied', *Englische Studien* xxxix 7 f. and Jente 315-22. *Ȝealdor*, however, occurs once elsewhere in a non-magical sense, cf. BT *Supplement galdor* (1).

fyrnsynn 347. The meaning of the first element of this nonce word is doubtful. BT translate 'sins of ancient times', and with this may be compared other compounds in *fyrn-*, such as *fyrnþeorc* (cf *Crist* 579 and *Andreas* 1410). The BT *Supplement*, however, takes *fyrn-* as a spelling of *firen*, thus forming a tautological compound, with which may be compared *firenbealu* (*Crist* 1275) and *firensynniȝ* (*Crist* 1378). Whilst the latter interpretation is perhaps slightly the more probable, either meaning would give good sense in the context.

oferhyȝd 424. This word with only two exceptions (see BT) has the sense of sinful pride, and is never used of ordinary heroic pride. Frequently it is used to translate the Latin *superbia*, the term for the greatest of the Seven Deadly Sins. For examples, see M. W. Bloomfield, *The Seven Deadly Sins* 252. The occurrence in *Juliana* is a good example of its use in this Christian technical sense.

sunsciene 229. This nonce word is unusual in that the first element in a compound rarely forms an object of metaphorical comparison. But cf *ælfscieno* (*Genesis* 1827, 2731, and *Judith* 14). Cf *Juliene* (Royal MS) 403-4, 'hire nebscheft schininde al as schene as þe sunne' (d'Ardenne p. 46).

þraȝmæl 344. The translation provided by BT 'from time to time' is weak both here and at *Andreas* 1230. In the latter Grein and Trautmann have suggested reading *traȝmælum* for metrical reasons, which, if accepted, would indicate an analogical emendation in *Juliana*. Grein's contention, however, that the alliteration must fall on the adverbial noun in preference to the verb *teon* is too dubious to justify the emendation in the *Andreas*. Some other explanation of the word in *Juliana* must therefore be sought. In view of New English 'throe' for which the NED can supply no satisfactory etymological development, and the fact that both in this compound and also sometimes when used as a separate word (e.g. *Juliana* 464) *þraʒ* appears to require the meaning 'distress', 'pain', it may at least be conjectured that it did possess this meaning, and that 'throe' developed from it. Whether *þráʒ* should be connected with *þréaʒan*, *þréa*, and in particular *þrapu*, and an original variant with a long vowel be postulated, or whether this meaning was simply a semantic development from the ordinary sense 'time' (i.e. time 7 time of distress 7 distress, cp a similar development of meaning in *stund* [NED stound]), remains open to doubt. Brooks suggests 'Time and time again' for *Andreas* 1230.

pinburʒ 83. Gollancz and Strunk read *pinburʒ*: joyous city. The word occurs five times in all but in no instance can the length of the vowel be determined on metrical evidence. The interpretation of Gollancz and Strunk is supported by the occurrence of the word with the probable meaning of 'joyful city' in Psalm cxxvii, 2 (*Psalms*, ed. Thorpe, p. 384). The number of analogous compounds with *pin*, however (e.g. *pinærn*, *pinsele*, etc), and the exact parallel in *meduburʒ* suggest very strongly that the vowel here should be long.

pyrd 38, 538. The word occurs only twice in *Juliana*, in each instance in the sense of 'what happens', though with a variation in emotional connotation. In all its occurrences in Cynewulf's poetry (except for *Elene* 1047, where it is equivalent to the will of God), *pyrd* has its weakened sense of an event as it is seen by man, instead of referring to some supernatural power or force which is the cause of events. By an odd inconsistency, however, the word could convey either the idea of happiness or disaster. The former arose from the fairly common identification of *pyrd* with the divine will in Old English religious poetry (cf Alfred's translation of the *de Consolatione Philosophiæ*), and the latter from the continued use of it in the Christian period in *Beowulf*, etc, as a poetic personification of the unavoidable course of disastrous events constantly seen in the world. In *Juliana*, as in *Fates of the Apostles* 42, but unlike many instances in the *Elene*, *pyrd* is used of a disastrous event, and its usage at l. 538 is purely in the heroic convention. At l. 33, however, the word appears to be used ambiguously, perhaps poised between the two connotations, for it might either mean 'the disastrous event to Eleusius (that Juliana rejected his love)', or 'the glorious fact (from the Christian point of view) that Juliana rejected the love of Eleusius'.

Scinlac 214. *Scin-* (originally connected with the verb 'shine') has an early meaning of 'phantom'. Whilst this meaning survives occasionally in *scin* and its compounds in Old English, like other words with magical associations, it came to be used specifically of the devil and his supernatural powers. *Scin, Scinna*, for instance, is a fairly common synonym for the devil (e.g. *Whale* 31, *Christ and Satan* 72), and *scinlac* occurs frequently in later saints' lives with the sense of sorcery worked by the devil or his agents, cf *scingelacum, Andreas* 766; in the *Metres of Boethius* xxvi, 74, it is used of Circe's powers. Since in *Juliana* the nature of the devil's threatened vengeance is unclear, though it would not seem to involve sorcery, the meaning of *scinlac* is perhaps the more general one of 'diabolical power'. For a full discussion of *scin* and its compounds see Jente pp. 155–61.

Woma 576 (and **hildewoma** 136, 663). This is one of the most interesting and puzzling words in Old English. All the evidence normally sufficient for establishing the meaning of a word is available: its etymology is known and it survives in at least six different contexts; nevertheless its meaning is disputable. Its associations are with battle, winter, dreams, daybreak and the Last Judgment. The original meaning is noise and Omi was one of the names of Oðinn, 'a personification of the wind as the voice of God' (Cleasby-Vigfusson). The semantic development suggested by Miss Gradon (note to *Elene* 19) of noise > noise of battle and noise > harbinger > revelation, though it accounts for all the occurrences of the word in the *Elene*, is not quite adequate for the interpretation of the uses in *Juliana*, in all of which there is a suggestion of something elusive and frightening. It may be tentatively suggested that an early meaning was 'sound of terror or of mystery' and that the emphasis then came to fall on the ideas of awe and fear. The word never occurs in prose.

Printed and bound by CPI Group (UK) Ltd, Croydon, CR0 4YY

13/04/2025

14656571-0003